Worth the Walk

Katie M. Schneider

burning soul press

Paperback ISBN: 978-1-964924-22-9
Hardcover ISBN: 978-1-964924-21-2
eBook ISBN: 978-1-964924-23-6

This is a work of nonfiction. The events and conversations in this memoir are portrayed to the best of the author's memory. In some instances, names and identifying details have been changed to protect the privacy of individuals. Dialogue and scenes may have been re-created or compressed for narrative flow. Any resemblance to actual persons, living or dead, is coincidental and unintentional unless explicitly stated by the author.

This book is intended for informational and inspirational purposes only. The author and publisher assume no responsibility for actions taken by readers based on the content herein.

Part One

The Roots of Pain

Shame, someone I used to know well
It became me, in all my forms
Carried into the day, into the night
Almost suffocating
When I ran from it, I ran to fear
Fear became my home
But why?
What is a life if you only have fear?
Sadness, it's the only version I could find
Tears, fading into the pores of my skin
This is who I am, who I was
Every piece of me broken into something
    smaller
Looking for its perfect place, searching
Until it was there, looking back through a
    mirror of light
It was me. The one I've been searching for

The hand I now hold, while it holds my heart
Every broken piece now has its place
A place where shame doesn't grow
A place where fear has no existence
A place where sadness can't breathe
Me. I am that place

Chapter One

I can still feel the scratchy and tough fibers of our family's 80s green shag carpet, nervously picking at it as my parents gathered us all in the living room before we went to school. My siblings and I gathered shoulder to shoulder, feeling our stiff tan couch creak beneath us as we sat down. The sun was just starting to peek through the windows as it rose that morning. I was only five years old and had just started my school year in kindergarten.

My dad spoke first, his voice cracking as he said the words: "Your mom and I are getting a divorce." I quickly stared back at those same carpet fibers again. The air felt heavy, like it was pressing on my chest. The news hit us like a ton of bricks as we sat there, shocked and silent. We all felt it was coming, but you could never quite prepare yourself for that kind of moment.

For months, they said they needed to talk, then disappeared into their bedroom, shutting us out from everything when they shut the door. My brother, sister, and I would sneak to their door and try to listen. We knew there was something going on that they weren't telling us about.

After delivering the news, they asked us a question that would shock each of us: which parent do you want to live with? When they asked us to choose whom to live with, I whispered, "I want both of you," tears blurring my vision as I clung to the couch. My siblings had answered quickly, their voices steady, but mine trembled as I hoped my response might make them change their minds. How could I even start to comprehend what was about to all happen?

The weight of their decision didn't hit me fully until later, but even at that moment, I felt an ache I couldn't quite name. Looking back, I see how those moments and those following planted seeds of doubt—about my worth, my safety, and whether I was truly loved. It was a question that would linger for years, shaping my relationships and how I viewed myself.

My parents worked out an agreement in court, and it was decided that my siblings and I would live primarily with our dad and stay with our mom every other weekend. This arrangement might seem surprising, especially at the time this was, when the mother would usually get primary custody of the kids in a situation like this. In hindsight, this probably saved me and my siblings from even more trauma than we were about to endure. I didn't realize this at the time, but it was the beginning of the last positive memories I would ever have of my mom.

It was like having two different moms: the one she was before she left, and the one who showed up afterward. The person she was before she left my dad was so calm—what I would consider a free spirit in a lot of ways, easy-going and someone I felt very safe with. I can still see her wavy black hair, deep brown eyes, and her pale porcelain skin. Her eyes could tell you any story, her emotions an open book. She had a wonderful way of smiling through her eyes when she'd laugh. I savor those memories of her because that would not be the mom I would end up having for the rest of my life. I can barely remember the mom I had those first five years.

As the divorce moved forward, my mom quickly began to move on with her new life. One she had been living secretly for some time. I didn't come to find this out until much later in life, but she had developed a gambling problem, spending her days in the dark corners of the poker tables. She even went to great lengths to take money from her own mother, since she was the custodial caregiver for her once she was placed in a nursing home. She was on a path of destruction, deceiving every single person in her life. She had been taking out loans to fuel her gambling problem and putting them in my dad's name while they were still married.

My mom's new life was a revolving door of boyfriends who used her for a place to live and spend the little money she had. She started drinking and partying a lot all on top of her growing gambling addiction.

I can't help but see it as her unhealed trauma catching up with her. She was one of the oldest amongst eight siblings, and her dad died suddenly when she was in her early twenties. It forced her to step up and help her mom take care of her younger siblings, making her grow up faster than she planned. She met my dad right around this time and he also stepped up in so many ways to be there for my mom and her family.

I believe my mom moved from raising one family to having her own, and the reality of missing the part of her life where she could be carefree with little responsibility started kicking in. With a husband and three young kids to care for, she wasn't happy and decided to start down a dark path that would end up completely changing the course of her life.

Unfortunately for me, these would end up being the core memories I have with her as a child. It was like she disappeared and transformed into someone who felt like a complete stranger to me. I desperately wish I could see her that way still, but her constantly choosing her addictions instead of her kids tarnished that quickly.

When she moved out of our family home, I would spend my weekends with her watching her drink at the bar while I played endless hours of arcade games with buttons covered in heavy smoke residue and remnants of greasy bar food. I can still taste and smell the stale bar popcorn I would fill up on throughout the course of the day.

At times it was fun getting to drink as much soda as a kid could possibly want, eating fried bar food for almost every meal, and getting endless rolls of quarters to play at the video game machines, but only if she won enough money on pull tabs to supply them. She would let me open all the pull tabs for her and I would get such a thrill when I'd open a winner, and she would cheer so loudly. There would be a quick moment when that spark in her eyes would return. She was just happy she could afford to continue drinking for the night. I actually thought to myself: "This is the best!" But I didn't realize how destructive it was until a night the cops were called on us.

My sister Nicole and I were with my mom for the weekend. My mom and her boyfriend went into the bar and had us stay in the car that was parked in the back alley. My mom opened the car door and whispered to us as her breath cradled her face like a wave of smoke, "We will only be ten minutes, stay here and don't move." Her eyes failed to meet ours in her encounter. As we sat there, cuddled together in the back seat, it started to get cold as the night drew in. All you could see were the bright colors of the neon bar signs outside and a glimpse of the bar jukebox music loudly playing inside. Luckily, someone saw us by ourselves as they were leaving and called the police.

My mom came outside to talk to the police, and she didn't seem concerned one bit about what had just happened. This wasn't a situation the mother I had previously would've ever let happen, and the shift in her character became more evident in this one situation. Her ability to see the liability of her actions was now completely nonexistent. I was scared, but I didn't fully realize just how much she was neglecting us when we were with her. This was when it was apparent that she wasn't just drinking for fun anymore. She had a problem. She was an alcoholic.

It was in that moment that I knew if we lived with my mom, it would end up steering our lives in a horrible direction. Having three young kids of my own now, I can't imagine putting my own children in a situation like that and it being at the hands of the one person in the entire world that should be protecting her kids at all costs. The severity of the situation and what it could have been is terrifying.

Her drinking had seemingly become her number one priority. There was a weekend she was supposed to have us, and she called my dad and asked if he would keep us. She even said she would pay him if she had to. He still pushed to have us go with her because he felt it was important for us to see her as much as possible. Not even an hour into our visit, my sister called my dad to come back and pick us up. When he arrived at her house, my mom was dressed up to go to a party. This was the reason she didn't want to have us for the weekend—she couldn't imagine missing out on a party or reason to drink in exchange for two nights with her own kids.

Even with these situations occurring and despite my dad's efforts, the court maintained the original custody arrangement. As a result, I spent my time with my mom sitting at bars for hours before being driven home by her or one of her intoxicated boyfriends. Once home, arguments would inevitably erupt. I would lie on her dirty, cigarette smoke-covered couch in the living room, crying myself to sleep as I listened to the fights unfold. It wasn't just yelling that I heard. For years, I witnessed the violence—each slap, punch, and kick she endured—and I would pray the blows weren't severe enough to silence her. When that happened, I knew it was an especially terrible night.

There was one fight that escalated pretty badly. She was dating a man that would end up being a part of her life for a really long time and he unfortunately had a bad habit of beating my mom to the point of her almost dying, multiple times. Once he made me watch him beat her. He told me, "Remember this. It's what happens when you are nothing." I was so scared of this man. He had the darkest eyes that showed pure evil when you'd look into them. He'd walk around with his fists always clenched, waiting for the next thing that would set him off. I could never bring myself to tell my dad what was happening when I was there. I was terrified that if I did, he would get in trouble, and I would have to go stay with my mom and he would end up hurting me too. Learning this coping skill at a young age wasn't healthy for me. It caused me to not advocate for myself when I needed to. I felt completely helpless. I couldn't protect her, and I felt so guilty feeling—like I just sat back and watched her suffer.

These events were unwanted fragments beginning to shape me as a person. I had always craved a strong sense of security. I don't like being put in positions where I feel like I'm unsafe with someone else. This was the first of the many cracks that began the process of completely breaking me.

I spent so many nights pleading to my mom with tears rolling down my cheeks to please just stop drinking. She would look at me, but her eyes were no longer the ones I remembered. It was like I was looking into a vacant soul. They were empty and unforgiving. The mom I had was no longer there. I would whisper to her as I cried to please just leave her boyfriend, to just spend time being my mom again. You could hear the pain pouring out of me with every word. I had lost the person who I felt closest to in this world. The one I felt so loved by. But her alcohol addiction took over her and she continuously chose everything besides her own kids. Years later, I realized these moments taught me to associate love with instability and fear, shaping every relationship I'd have in my future.

I started to blame myself for her leaving, thinking that I did something to make her not want to love me anymore. A fear of abandonment started to surface. This was the first of many masks I would wear throughout my life, trying to hide the hurt and shame I carried from the rest of the world. If my own mom couldn't love me enough to stay in my life, why would anyone else? Questions that a young child should never have to ask themselves.

Chapter Two

I would watch my dad through the gap in the garage door on winter nights, the orange glow of his cigarette illuminating his face in the darkness. His shoulders hunched as he leaned against his messy tool bench, silent words forming on his lips that I could never quite hear. The sharp scent of motor oil mixed with tobacco smoke created a bitter perfume that, even now, brings back the image of my dad back then, trying to hold himself together in the only space he felt safe enough to break in. I'd quietly walk back into the house wishing it would be me that he would talk to, so we could both share the pain that was in our hearts.

My dad, Jack, is one of the most important people in my life today. I have so much appreciation for the sacrifices he made for my siblings and me after my parents' divorce. I didn't always feel that way though. My early memories of my dad were like puzzle pieces that weren't all put together quite yet. Each piece carefully crafted, waiting for me to find its place, one by one. He would come home exhausted from work or after weekends spent in a deer stand hunting and bonding with my brother. In many ways, he was like a stranger who had suddenly become our primary caregiver. It took years until all the pieces came together to form a complete picture for me.

I spent a large portion of my life blaming him for the life we had growing up. It took me a long time, but as I've worked on unpacking all this by digging deep into my past, I realized that the blame I placed on him was completely unnecessary.

Some of the only early memories I have of my dad outside of his work and hunting is that he was quick to yell, accompanied by a temper. I struggled a lot when we first started living primarily with him. He too was struggling, though.

I can't fathom the stress my dad carried at the time after finding out everything my mom had done. Imagine your marriage ending, losing the house you once shared, and struggling to pay back a tremendous amount of debt that wasn't even yours—all while you raise three young kids by yourself. I commend my dad for doing what he did coming out of that, but I wish I would've seen this sooner. I understand why he didn't tell us all the details of their divorce at the time. He didn't want to add any further negativity to our relationship with our mom. It says a lot about his character that he chose not to tarnish what little relationship we did have left with her. He was so stressed out those years following the divorce, just trying to get us above water again. He was working a job that barely kept us afloat most of the time.

One thing I am very thankful my dad did was move us to a new city farther away from our mom. We were living in a larger city that once was a safe place to raise your kids and was now becoming a city full of crime. I remember the first time we drove to our new home, seeing the sign with a population count just a fraction of what we were coming from. The quietness felt somewhat safe though, as we drove through the little town immersed with small businesses, modest homes, and friendly people who knew everyone by their first name. It felt like another world to me. We pulled up to a small gray house with a dirt driveway in a tucked away neighborhood. This was my new home. I saw kids running in the streets, joyfully screaming and laughing. They all stopped and carefully studied the new family that was moving into the old vacant house that needed a lot of work. Each kid's eyes meeting mine as I slouched down in the back seat hoping to not be seen. My nerves began to show their face as I quickly realized that I was going to feel like an outsider, being the new girl in town where friendships had been formed since diapers, and I was going to have to find where I fit into it all. But it gave us all a fresh start we desperately needed.

It was hard at first, as our new routine emerged slowly. I would wake up most days to a quiet house with little evidence of my dad's morning routine before he left the house by six each day. His half empty coffee cup on the counter next to the sink, a note that would say, "Love your guts," that he quickly wrote before heading out the door. I would return home to that same empty house after school. My dad traveled back to our old city for his job at the water treatment facility, driving an hour each way.

As I sat and watched TV after school, I would sit on the ledge of the window and wait to see his little turquoise truck drive around the corner. He would pull into the driveway with his windows down, a cigarette in his hand, and you could hear the blast of oldies music playing on the radio. He would shut off the ignition, but he wouldn't get out of the car right away. He'd sit there for a moment, staring blankly ahead. It was almost as if he was searching for any ounce of energy he had left to come home to his three kids needing him. He would climb out of his truck carrying his coffee thermos and lunch bag, wearing his tan uniform and large clunky work boots. He would come into the house fully exhausted. He'd walk up to our fridge, and he would carefully empty his pockets placing his wallet, pack of cigarettes, and car keys on top of the fridge. You could feel the weight of the world being lifted off him as he placed them in the same spot as he always did, one by one. Before he did anything else I would see him already standing at the stove, stirring the boiling water full of spaghetti noodles. He would ask for help by carefully teaching me how to test if spaghetti was done by throwing it against the refrigerator door to see if it would stick. This became my favorite part of spaghetti night. These small moments—watching him craft meals from scratch that made us feel cared for—became the building blocks of our new normal.

After dinner we would often spend our evenings eating my dad's favorite snack—ice cream. We'd gather together in our small but cozy living room recliners, surrounding our TV that was small but didn't ever bother us. I'd giggle between each bite of my vanilla ice cream covered in chocolate syrup, listening to my dad's belly laugh at all of "Tim the Tool Man Taylor" jokes on Home Improvement. It was my dad's favorite show, and I can still picture him mimicking Tim Allen's grunting sounds and then laughing at himself afterwards. Hearing his loud laugh made me so happy, it was some of the only moments I would see him smile at that time in our lives. You could see the cracked wrinkles around his eyes when he would laugh. And his newly graying hair that was starting to show in his beard.

I never felt like I could express to him how I was truly feeling on the inside. I held everything in. I didn't want to be another reason he was stressed out. I did everything to not be a problem. Oftentimes, while I would lay in bed at night with tear-stained pillowcases from the many nights I'd cry before, releasing all the pain I was holding onto. Telling myself stories of a life I pictured for myself but seemed impossible to obtain.

I would envision myself with another family. Picturing a big house I'd come home to after school every day, running from the bus with a smile from ear to ear on my face. Barreling through the front door to greet a mom who couldn't wait to hear all of my excitement from the day. We'd sit and talk about what happened at school while I ate a snack she carefully crafted for my arrival. Laughing at the silly things I would say as she'd start making dinner for our family. We'd play outside with my dad when he got home from work until we'd hear the blissful "dinner's ready!" from my mom. We'd gather around the table and each take our turns sharing all the discoveries we made that day. Ending our night with cuddles on the couch while we'd read stories before bed. Each parent would tuck me in and tell me how much I was loved. Then, I'd fall asleep only to wake up to another reality. Taking on another day of silencing myself and my pain.

What that ended up doing was teach me to believe that if you don't express your emotions, you won't drive people away. I didn't want another person to leave me, so I did everything I could to not be a problem. What I really needed was for someone to step up and see the help not only I myself needed, but my siblings as well.

My brother knew more about my parents' divorce than my sister and I, which I'm sure took a toll on him. He distanced himself from my mom right away, and I don't blame him. The divorce caused my sister to rebel a lot and most of the time, she was fighting with my dad over how many weeks she would be grounded this time for things she would get caught doing, like sneaking out of the house in the middle of the night or smoking cigarettes with her friends after school. He would take his pen and write "Nicole on house arrest," with an arrow from the start to finish on our little paper calendar hanging on the fridge.

My dad just didn't have the capacity to do more than he was doing. It wasn't that he didn't want to or that he didn't care about us. I think he clearly saw how the dynamic of our mom leaving us and her alcoholism was impacting us all in our own ways. However, through no fault of his own, he didn't have the bandwidth to help us to the extent we probably all needed. There are so many examples of things I couldn't see at the time because of the hurt and anger I was holding on to—the efforts he made to ensure we had home cooked meals to eat every day, clothes to wear, activities to join, money in our school lunch accounts. He truly provided everything we physically needed. We were in a home that was safe and not surrounded with endless liquor bottles, abusive partners, and empty refrigerators. Things so many people pray for. Instead of seeing this I spent my time and energy comparing my life to everyone around me, often leaving me feeling like I was never going to be good enough for anyone, because of the situation I came from.

These were fragments that continued to build new layers in my life where my emotional safety would be tested. I certainly didn't love myself enough to express my needs. I focused so much on what I could do differently to make people love me. I had spent so much time blaming myself for my mom leaving, convincing myself I was the problem. In turn, I would alter my behavior, personality, emotions, etc. to cater to whoever I needed to. I would say things that I thought people wanted to hear instead of what I was truly feeling or thinking. I liked certain things because my friends did, hoping this would cause them to like me more. I avoided asking to do certain activities because I knew it was too expensive and it would stress my dad out. I acted happy, even when I was drowning in sadness. I did these things with my family, friends, teachers, everyone. I don't think I ever had a sense of who I truly was for the entirety of my childhood. Something I'm still learning—who I am to this very day.

This ended up creating issues for myself in my future relationships. I ignored red flags and compromised my own needs because I didn't want to drive people away. I tolerated behavior that was often less than the bare minimum. Telling myself if I spoke up and asked for more, they would just end up leaving me. The abandonment wound in me ran so deep I lived my life terrified of losing anyone I loved.

I was so guarded with my heart because of this. I had no way of knowing how to regulate all the emotions and trauma I was holding on to. I learned to mask my emotions throughout my life and felt like I was two completely different people. The one that I held inside for no one else to see, and the one I showed the world full of masks hiding her truths.

Back then, I wish I had the capacity and awareness I do now, so I could've worked through all this much earlier in my life. But then again, it's why I am the woman I am in this exact moment, and I don't take that for granted one bit. I think my biggest learning from all of this is that sometimes when bad things happen to us, the broken parts of us look for someone to blame. It helps us dissect the messiness and we think we understand it better. We get validation through thinking: "I feel this way because this person did this to me." But sometimes we have to meet people where they are at. This is what I needed to do with my dad while I was growing up. Yes, I needed more from him, but he truly did everything he was capable of at that time. It wasn't for a lack of care or desire to give everything for his kids. He was shattered and trying to put himself back together all while trying to hold it all together for us. Now that I'm a mom myself, I can't imagine being in that exact same position that he was in. It would absolutely break me, and I don't know if I could survive the way he did.

This is a thank you to him. It wasn't until I had my own kids that I saw my dad's sacrifices differently. He didn't fail us; he saved us.

Chapter Three

Sunlight streamed through floor-to-ceiling windows, painting warmth across my friend's living room. As we sat watching Sunday football, her mom absently ran her fingers through my hair—a gesture so maternal it made my throat clench. We talked about nothing special—school, sports, friends—but in that moment, I felt what home should feel like. Tears filled my eyes as I savored this borrowed slice of motherhood. It was these moments that made returning to my own house feel like stepping into a shadow.

When our family first moved to this small town, my dad met my now stepmom and they ended up building a house together after a few years. But that house never truly felt like home. I often felt like a guest, and I clung to the normalcy I found in my friends' homes. If I wasn't at work or school, I would often find excuses to leave. I felt more at home when I was anywhere else.

I wouldn't say blending our two families together was easy by any means. We went through many years of growing pains, with my sister and stepmom's relationship being the focal point of those tensions. My stepmom has two daughters that are very close in age to my brother and sister. There were some differences there that caused friction amongst everyone. It caused a divide between the two families, and my sister often bore the blame for many of the deeper family issues. It created friendship issues with my step-siblings and caused a divide between them so big that love was lost somewhere in the space that was created.

I was only in second grade at this time, so I don't know everything that truly happened, but what it felt like was that my sister was always the one doing things wrong. She wasn't perfect and she rebelled a lot as she worked through her own emotions because of our mom. I felt in the middle of it all at times because I wanted to protect my sister and stand up for her. I knew exactly what it felt like for others to not show up for me when I needed it, so I felt like the least I could do was offer her that. I felt somewhat obligated to her, even when I didn't fully understand what was happening. I think this just went with the territory of being the youngest. I wanted to feel included and be liked by not only my own siblings, but my stepsiblings as well. At the same time, I felt protective of my sister. No one else was stepping up to do this, so it felt like my only option at the time.

Over the years I didn't agree with how my stepmom treated my sister. And I was even more frustrated when I felt that my dad just sat back and let it happen. There were so many times I just wanted to scream at the top of my lungs while sitting at the dinner table, "Why are you doing this to her? Why can't you just love us? You know what we have been through." It was crazy to me that this dynamic was the case for our family and being the youngest, I was the one who had to live in that environment the longest.

Because of this, once my dad and stepmom moved in together, I truly never felt like I was comfortable in my own home growing up. I felt like I was constantly walking on eggshells, worrying about the next wrong thing I would do. I felt like a guest in my own house. I felt ashamed even walking to the fridge to get something to eat, thinking I was being watched and judged the entire time. This drove me even further away from my dad and I would do anything to not have to be home if I could. So, I was in sports year-round to make sure I had things to do after school and spent a ton of time at my friends' houses where I honestly felt more at home there than I did at my own house. But then I would have to go back to my house, and I would walk around feeling like I was always holding my breath. I was a ticking time bomb. I felt like eyes were always on me. I'd be at the dinner table talking about my day or something that happened at school and I would catch my stepmom watching me as I told my story. Her eyes narrowed at me with judgment and skepticism, like every story I told was a web of lies. I can't recall many times at that stage of my life where there was a smile on her face when I was in her presence. It made me feel like the smallest person in the world. I didn't matter and I was never going to be enough for this person to love me like her own. An extension of the love that was lacking in my relationship with my own mother. Something that was so familiar to me but was always in the back of my mind lingering with every move I made.

As I was getting ready for middle school one day, I saw it as I exited my room and walked along the hallway past my parents' bedroom door. The Curve perfume bottle sat on my stepmom's vanity like a blue jewel, its promise of belonging too tempting to resist. Every girl at school wore it

21

—that distinctive scent that marked you as part of the in-crowd. One small spray felt like putting on invisible armor, a shield of normalcy. When I got home that afternoon, my dad confronted me: "Did you use your stepmom's perfume this morning before you went to school? You didn't even ask her if that was okay." His voice sharp with accusation, frustration hanging on every word. I realized I'd never be allowed even this small piece of fitting in. The same perfume that my stepsisters could've borrowed freely became contraband in my hands, another reminder that I existed on the margins of this family. I was so shocked that she even knew I used one small spray of her perfume hours prior.

After getting yelled at I went back to my room, the only place I felt safe, and just sat there and cried. I dreamed of having a relationship with her that we could share perfume, I could borrow her fun makeup, and she would do my hair for me. But that's not even close to what I had. I had so much shame feeling like I was the outsider in the family and not good enough for her. It was like she was always just waiting for me to get caught doing something else wrong so I would get in trouble.

Then there would be moments that would give me a glimmer of hope, that love did exist for me in her heart. Every year for my birthday she would make her famous pink cake from scratch like she did for everyone else in the family. For that tiny moment, I would watch her as she frosted every inch of the cake so carefully. Paying attention to all the intricate details that led her to a flawless masterpiece. It was a small gesture that felt genuine. I would close my eyes and hold on so tightly to the moment. Hoping more of these would come along. Memories I would cherish and store away for times I needed the reminder that it wasn't hard to love me.

Despite these moments of glorified care, every single day as I went through middle and high school, I would avoid interactions with her and my dad. I kept myself busy with friends and I felt like my own dad and stepmom wouldn't even know the real me if they saw how I was when I wasn't at home. I didn't want any of my friends knowing the truth, so I put on a façade about my life. I used humor as a distraction and a way to get people to like me.

If you talked to any of my friends growing up, I think a lot of them would've said I was the life of the party, always up for a good time and constantly doing things to make others laugh. It was the only sliver of validation I ever had that I was liked by someone, because every other part of my life felt like I was just a disappointment and not worthy of the love I know I truly deserved. I would often wander the halls at school closely examining all the name brand clothing the other girls gleefully showed off. I would look down at the same sweater I wore on repeat covered in shame and embarrassment because I couldn't afford to buy the things everyone else was wearing. I would hold tears back as my friends would recap their weekends filled with shopping trips to the mall with their moms, stopping at a fun restaurant to eat lunch as the mountain of bags filled with new clothes and jewelry surrounded them in the booth.

What I really needed was an outlet to help me see a perspective beyond what I was capable of at the time. I was covered in masks of anger, resentment, and blame. All stemming from a deep-rooted hurt that I would've done anything to escape.

Growing up, I wasn't someone who was ever strong in

my faith, but the dynamic of my life at that time was what drove my anger towards God more than I ever realized. All the adults in my life were not guiding me to Him. My dad wasn't someone who I would say was strong in his relationship with God while I was growing up. The irony of my stepmom working at our church while our home felt so devoid of Christian love wasn't lost on me.

Each Sunday, we'd go to church as a family, then come home to an environment where judgment replaced grace, where conditional love was the only kind offered. It created a spiritual paradox I couldn't reconcile—if this was God's love in action, I wanted no part of it. My faith withered in the shadow of this hypocrisy, leaving a void that would take decades to fill. It made me question the little amount of faith I had even more. I would think to myself often, "Why is God punishing me all the time?" I truly felt like he wanted me to suffer my entire life.

Reflecting on those earlier years of my life, I see how each moment chipped away at my self-worth. I became an expert at hiding my feelings, perfecting a mask of indifference to shield myself from the judgment I feared. But the shame stayed, burrowing deep and shaping how I saw myself for years to come. That pain that I sat in for so long ended up shaping me as I went into my adulthood and impacted how I viewed life in its entirety, putting me on a path of constant self-sabotage, attaching myself to any form of external validation I could find and not knowing at all who I was or the person I was meant to be. I was completely lost.

Writing about this relationship now is something that is hard for me to do. A few years ago in therapy, my stepmom was actually one of the people my current therapist asked me to write a letter to as a between session assignment. I was kind of surprised at the time because I didn't feel like that relationship had that big of an impact on me and what I was trying to work through at the time. However, it ended up showing me that there was a lot of unresolved hurt that I needed to unpack. I have spent a lot of time reflecting on my own accountability with all this and how I could have shown up differently back then. I've resolved a lot of the resentment I was holding on to about my past and my upbringing. Now that I've learned more about my parents' divorce and the struggles my dad was facing, he was completely broken and my stepmom was one thing that brought him any ounce of happiness. And I'm so glad that they are still together and he has her in his life.

The way I felt back then is not the same reality I have with her today. She embraces me with love and care when I walk through the front door with my kids in tow. She loves them in the midst of the chaos that follows us. She listens as I tell her the updates in my life and the struggles that come with it. It almost feels like both of our hearts have softened since that time in my life. There have been learnings along the way, and I truly feel like our relationship has grown immensely over the years. There were times I didn't feel I could turn to her, or even my dad, and they are usually one of the first phone calls I make when I have something exciting to share or I'm having a hard day. A space where I used to feel so lost, now has become a new sense of home for me.

Chapter Four

The night before graduation, I stood in my bedroom, my fingers tracing the edge of my acceptance letter to college in North Dakota—a place so far from home it might as well have been another planet. The faint sounds of my dad and stepmom's television drifted from the living room as I whispered to my reflection, "Just a few more months and you're free." Freedom tasted sweet on my tongue. But I had no idea I was simply trading one prison for another—one I had built for myself brick by brick with the weight of masks I'd grown too comfortable wearing.

As I entered my senior year of high school and my graduation approached, I couldn't wait to move out, escaping the prison I had held myself captive in. But I would just end up running further away from the truth within myself.

It was at this time in my life that I started to distance myself more and more from my mom. My visits to her became less and less. The forced phone calls filling her in on all the intricate details of my life dwindled as the prior years passed. When I would see her, which wasn't often, it was like talking to a complete stranger. Her addiction to alcohol had now spread to drugs as well. The black wavy hair she once had was now brittle and completely gray. Her eyes were empty, lined with large dark circles underneath them. Her face was usually covered in bruises from her last fight with her boyfriend. One conversation with her ended up being one of the last times I ever saw her. It made me realize having a normal relationship with her was more than likely never going to happen.

My brother, sister, and I went to visit her for Christmas. Her apartment was a jungle of neglect—dozens of plants crowded every surface, competing for space and light, their leaves yellowing at the edges like her graying hair. Every surface told a story of decay: overflowing ashtrays created mounds of cigarette butts, each one marking another hour lost to addiction. The furniture, more than likely salvaged from roadsides, carried the ghosts of previous owners in its cigarette burns and mysterious stains.

As we all sat down, she asked us question after question, trying to catch up on the tiny details that filled our lives. There was one point during the conversation where she looked right at me and said, "Remember when Mom moved us out of Burnsville during high school and you were so angry at her?" I made quick eye contact with my brother, confused, and turned back to her and asked, "What are you talking about?" And she repeated it again, not even realizing what she was saying. But in that moment, it was her eyes that haunted me most—when she called me Carrie, mistaking me for her sister, I saw no recognition flicker in those vacant pools. My mother had become a stranger who only shared my DNA. She didn't know who I was. Her own daughter. Tears filled my eyes as I told my brother and sister I was ready to go. I didn't know who she was anymore, and it was clear that she didn't know me either. I left that day with more anger brewing beneath the surface. I knew I couldn't continue to put myself through that, so I made the decision I wasn't going to have her in my life anymore.

In the months following I decided to call her before my high school graduation party. I could feel my voice shaking harder than my hands trying to hold the phone as I told her I didn't want her to come to the party. Her voice equally as shaky as she responded with a simple, "but why?" Two words that left me spiraling in anger. What did she mean *why*? Her inability to see how any of her actions over the years would lead to this was mind blowing. Confusion and hurt filled the words she shared with me after that, begging me to reconsider. It was like she was in my shoes all those times I would beg her to stop drinking. To snap out of the harsh reality of her drinking problem. I could hear myself as a child in the words that carried from one end of the phone to the other.

I made that decision once I realized how much hurt she was still causing me. She would commit to things she could never follow through with, further fueling my insecurities of abandonment and disappointment. Her inconsistency always left me wondering and second guessing everything she would tell me. I was always holding my breath for her next phone call or promised birthday gift that somehow never seemed to make it to me. She would never follow through with anything she committed to with me, and it made me question if I was ever going to be worthy of her love. All I wanted was for her to show up, but it was often overshadowed by disappointment that continued to consume me. I felt so strongly that she didn't deserve to celebrate such a big accomplishment in my life when she chose to not ever be there for me growing up. Cutting ties with Mom was supposed to feel like relief, but instead, it left a hollow ache. I wondered if I was abandoning her the way she had abandoned me.

After graduation I left for college in the cold state of North Dakota. Thinking I was going to have this amazing new life where no one knew the battles I had been facing and the broken parts that were holding me together. I was convinced I could be this new version of myself and leave the old broken one behind. College wasn't just parties and bars—it was my first taste of reinvention. In my freshman English class, I could be the insightful student, raising my hand without fear. In the dining hall, I could be the social butterfly, collecting friends like trading cards.

Each new role was a mask I wore perfectly, while underneath, the scared little girl wondered if anyone would love her if they saw behind the disguise. My dorm room became a stage where I performed 'normal' for an audience that never knew they were watching a play, but I was still wearing the many masks that I developed throughout my life. I was in complete denial with myself, not admitting that so much of the damage had been done but never dealt with. I was completely broken, and this would be the start of me realizing just how bad it was. I partied a lot, using alcohol to numb the reality I was in. But my friends didn't see that side of me, they saw this fun girl who was the first one to jump at the chance of fun. I continued to convince everyone around me that I was "fine"—oftentimes only showing the surface-level parts of me.

About a month after starting my freshman year, I met a guy that would end up being the first serious relationship I ever had. I was living in the co-ed dorms with my childhood friend Abbey, and we'd wander the different floors at night hoping to meet new friends. We stumbled upon his dorm room one night and they had invited a few people over to watch a football game. We happily joined and as I sat down, he immediately caught my eye. He was tall and athletic. The typical type I would go for at that time. He had the brightest smile that was impossible to ignore. You could tell he was immediately drawn to me too. I would catch him staring at me from across the room as I fell in conversation with everyone else around us.

At one point he finally had the courage to strike up a conversation with me. He was going to grab something to drink and asked if I wanted anything. As he brought me back something he sat down next to me. I could feel the flutters in my stomach as we started talking. I was so nervous and just wanted him to like me. We shared with each other all about where we grew up, what classes we were taking, etc. The usual getting to know someone conversation starters. As I listened carefully to each word that came out of his mouth, I loved that he grew up in a small farming town, played sports in high school, and seemed like he was really close with his family. He was the normal, steady guy I was looking for. Deep down, I was desperately looking for someone to love me. I craved security and hoped for someone who would bring me that, and it felt like all the things I was looking for at that time.

The next few weeks flew by as we spent every free minute we had together. Going out for dinners, catching a movie on a random Wednesday, sleeping in on a Sunday morning after going out with our friends the night before. I don't think I stopped smiling once in the months following. I felt like it was the first time someone loved me, and it gave me a sliver of hope that what I was looking for was out there. I could have a happily ever after, after all. I remember when I told him I loved him for the first time. Words that were hanging on the tip of my tongue for weeks before they saw the light of day. My hands sweating as I mustered up the courage to share something I didn't think I would ever get to. Desperate to have him say the same three words back. When I saw the smile grow across his face, I knew that he felt the same way. Something I felt I needed to earn throughout my life came so easily for the two of us. A place so unfamiliar to me that I didn't know the pressure it would build within me. I started to realize this relationship would unmask a lot of the wounds I was hiding behind, and I wasn't prepared to face what was left underneath them.

In this relationship, my fear of abandonment and feeling unworthy were easily triggered within me. We were both new to a serious relationship and didn't handle conflict well. I wanted to know this person wasn't going to leave so I went out of my way to self-sabotage. I would run from any form of conflict we would encounter, testing him to see if he would chase after me and stay. I wanted him to prove to me that he wasn't going to leave. After we would get into arguments, I would run to my sister's apartment or to a friend's dorm and wouldn't answer any of his phone calls or texts. The little girl within me thought this would bring him closer to me. That he would miss me and want to work things out. I was so broken in my thought process that I just wanted him to chase me, obsess over me. I was so immature in regulating my emotions I had no idea how much I was tearing the relationship apart by doing these things. But my actions were causing so many issues that it became impossible to stay in this relationship. We broke up after only six months of dating each other and I felt like my whole world was ending when that happened. It brought me right back to that little girl who questioned her worth through those around her. Once again someone was proving to me that I was hard to love. Not even seeing that I was the one projecting all these insecurities into my relationship over and over again.

When I was 20, I met a guy who was two years younger than me. This would end up being my next serious relationship. He had the brightest blonde hair, piercing sky-blue eyes, tan skin; I was completely smitten. He brought out a side of me that I hadn't encountered before. It was the most comfortable I had ever felt around a guy. I wasn't scared to share with him the trauma from my past and when that didn't make him run, I felt safe for the first time ever with a man. We fell hard and fast for each other, and I think it was a perfect portrayal of the phrase "young love." A lot of my friends questioned our age difference even though it was only two years. But at that stage of life, a two-year age gap felt like we were from two completely different worlds.

My friends and I were all turning 21 and starting to go out to the bars every weekend. And he was just starting out as a freshman in college and seemed like it was so far away from where I was in my life. Despite this, we wanted to be with each other no matter what anyone told us. I quickly fell in love with his family and felt like I fit right in. His mom and dad were so kind and welcoming, a feeling I craved for most of my life, and I loved his sisters. His parents never said it, but I think they both were concerned with the age difference at the time knowing I was one year out from graduating college and he was just starting out in his. This would end up being the reason we would break up down the road, but I can't help but think how much he did for me in that time of my life.

He was the first safe place I had ever encountered in a relationship. I was able to remove a lot of the masks I had been wearing all my life to hide my truths. There were nights he would stay awake with me, offering me empathy as I cried in his arms telling him the aches of my past. He understood why I was so afraid of people leaving me and he offered me the reassurance I needed that he wasn't going to just up and leave me like so many others did. We truly loved each other, and I believe that to this day. But that came with some unhealthy attributes as well.

We became so attached to each other that I distanced myself from my friends, my hobbies, school, you name it. I poured all of myself into this relationship, that without it, I didn't know who I was. I allowed our relationship to fill every crevice of energy that I consumed, and it became my entire identity. I used it to fill all the voids I had been carrying with me for most of my life. It was a hard realization when our relationship ended. Once again, I felt so alone. He brought me so much comfort by always being there and spending all my free time with him that when we broke up, I felt like I had no one. I had to rebuild my friendships again, start focusing back on school and getting ready to graduate.

Each relationship became a carefully choreographed dance of testing and running. I'd push boundaries, deliberately create chaos that felt familiar, then watch to see who would chase after me. Every argument became a testament to my worth—would they stay despite my manufactured drama, or would they prove what I already believed: that I was fundamentally unlovable? It was a self-fulfilling prophecy, my fear of abandonment becoming the very thing that drove people away. This would end up being a pattern in my relationships going forward. I had gotten to the point where I truly hated the person I was that I didn't feel like I deserved to be loved by anyone. I would tell myself if I left first, they couldn't hurt me. The dream I had of falling in love, getting married, and starting a family was slowly slipping through my fingertips as I went through relationship after relationship. I was so unaware of my destructiveness that I refused to see that I was mostly doing this to myself.

It was another lie I would tell myself—that without someone else, I didn't think being happy was possible. I was so broken that I thought someone else was the only way I was ever going to be happy. I would tell myself that if I find the right boyfriend, get a good job out of college, make a lot of money, that I would finally be happy. It didn't matter the inner battle I was constantly fighting. I couldn't see it. I thought to myself, if you never have to worry about being alone and you're in a good place financially, the rest of your life will be great. I was so focused on these external factors bringing me happiness, it's all I could think about. It's what I would look for in everything I did. If you just accomplish this, you will be happy. It was a cycle I repeated over and over again.

Sometimes I think about the girl I was back then, and I just want to go back and shake her. Walking around in a shell of this distinguished armor. Covering the parts I was so scared to share with the world, it was an invisible battle I fought within myself every single day.

If I could tell her anything, I would tell her to spend your twenties enjoying and exploring life. Learn to love yourself fully, seek adventure, make yourself whole again. Find that happiness within you so that you don't settle for less than you deserve. Reconnect with your faith in God.

However, I let the unhealed version of myself take the driver's seat, and it wouldn't be for a long time that I would realize all that. So off I went on this continued journey of seeking validation that I was good enough for anyone that I would encounter. Still wearing the masks of my past. One night as I stared at myself in the mirror, a reflection looked back that I didn't recognize anymore. I whispered to her and said, "Who are you trying to fool? Go find that girl you lost all those years ago—she needs you."

Part Two

The Storm Within

I found myself in the shadows of your mind
Buried beneath the memories that were met
    by the sun
I sat there, wondering how I became an over-
    cast in your heart?
My love for you pouring out from the cracks
    you created
Cracks that were so deep, not even the light
    could reach them
So many questions lined the inside of my
    mind
Searching for the truths you harbored
But the answers were never found
Until you became dust on this earth
Your words I had been searching for
Were left in the night, written with the ink of
    regret

Katie M. Schneider

Now I hold those, still in your shadows
That keep me held hostage to your forever
    truths

Chapter Five

It was the kind of cold that made your nose hairs freeze and your lungs ache with each breath—that's what I remember about the night I met him. Downtown Fargo had transformed into a ghost town, the usual college crowds thinned by the brutal weather. That's when he appeared, tall enough to block out the neon beer signs behind him, with a smile that promised warmth in this frozen landscape. This was the moment I would end up meeting my future husband.

We weren't complete strangers, but we had never officially met in the few years prior, even though we had a lot of mutual friends. He was tall, extremely smart, outgoing, and seemed like a really nice guy. We spent most of the night talking and flirting, my smile growing bigger as we talked over stale tap beers and too many rounds of shots. The noise of loud dance music, laughing friends, and glasses being dropped behind the bar seemed like they were so far away in that moment. His laugh was the only thing I could hear. We shared stories of the times we shared with friends at this exact same bar over the years, wondering how our paths had never crossed before. My heart was feeling hopeful for the first time in years. I knew this night wasn't going to be our last.

And I was right. At the end of the night we exchanged phone numbers, my hands shaking as I carefully typed each number one after the other hoping I didn't enter it in wrong. I left with butterflies in my stomach, anxiously awaiting his first phone call. Then a cloud of doubt came over me. The questions started lining up in my mind: "Why would someone so great be interested in someone like me? What do I have to offer him? Am I good enough for someone like that?" The fear of not being worthy changed the course of what was a night filled with fun and laughter to doubt, fear, and shame. The same feelings that were hard to escape most days.

To my surprise, he actually called me when he got home that night and we talked as the cold dark sky turned to a glisten of white as the sun touched its surface. From the start, I could tell that he had a good head on his shoulders and that he wasn't the typical college guy just trying to get my attention. He actually seemed interested in spending more time with me and getting to know me. Our early dates were low key, but I was enjoying my time with him and getting to know him more. He was studying engineering, so I knew he was smart. At times, it made me feel somewhat inferior. But he checked a lot of the boxes that I was looking for at the time. It was all I could dream of at that time for myself.

The first couple of months in a new relationship are always pretty easy, filled with all the excitement of spending time together and learning all the tiny details that have made this person who they are. So right away I don't think there were any concerns or red flags. He wanted to graduate, settle down, get married, and start a family. That to me was so important and I was so happy that we aligned in those parts of our lives. I knew early on that a life with him would give me a sense of security I had craved my whole life. He was responsible with money, trustworthy, had a good job lined up for when he graduated, and wanted a wife and kids. On paper, everything seemed perfect. However, there were warning signs from the beginning that I chose to ignore because I didn't want to let go of what a life with him would give me. It pains me to even write those words. The person I am now would have never compromised my deepest needs and desires in a partner for the sake of a sense of security in life. The things I thought mattered and would bring me happiness ended up being what blinded me from the harsh truth that was staring me right in the face.

After we graduated college, we moved back to the same area where he grew up. We spent the first six months in our new city living apart until we finally made the decision to buy our first house and move in together. I was so excited to start building a life that I had been dreaming of for as long as I could remember. I was savoring each thought of settling down together, getting married, and starting a family of our own. I had this sense of security that would whisper to me, "I'll never have to worry about being alone again." But there always seemed to be something in the way of us and our rela-tionship. We just never got to a point where we were in sync with one another. I was emotionally guarded and didn't feel fulfilled by him in that regard, feeling like if I showed any drop of emotion, it would drown him. Like my feelings were a burden he couldn't quite possibly carry, often telling me I was overreacting or being too emotional. This put tension on our physical relationship, and I think that weighed on the both of us. The lack of intimacy was glaring and blinding us as we navigated the crooked path we were walking. Never hand in hand. One always a little in front of the other, outpacing the other. It felt more like an uphill battle than a leisurely stroll through life together.

He wasn't someone that was easy to argue with. Being an engineer, he often approached everything as a black and white matter. The gray didn't exist, and any emotional feeling wasn't valid. His goal was to prove his point and win the argument. Nor did he give me space to feel understood and validate my feelings. I felt like I was being silenced from my own truths. It brought me back to when I was a little girl. Feeling helpless with my words. Knowing that when I would speak them, no one would listen. Telling my mom how she made me feel always fell on deaf ears, and my relationship wasn't any different.

I think we both knew this wasn't how you should feel in a relationship, but we both ignored the signs anyway. Because on paper, we had a great life. Good jobs, our own house, money in the bank. What else could you possibly need to be happy? Our relationship was the epitome of transactional. And we were just going through the motions, checking boxes along the way, but never truly embracing a level of intimacy a strong and healthy relationship needs in order to nurture itself into something special. Once again, here I was thinking that checking the boxes would equal a happy life. One I had so desperately wanted my entire life. All of the cracks in me leading up to this were wide open now, and yet I was still in complete denial. And based on the life I saw my mom living, I knew that my life would be good enough if I just continued on the path I had in front of me.

The gaps in our communication made me feel like we were worlds apart. Even at night when we would join one another in our small living room, we'd plant ourselves on separate couches. Our conversations barely surpassing the surface. Speaking completely different languages and trying to guess what the other one was saying. This made it difficult for me to express myself in fear of losing him and he seemed to have a hard time understanding emotions that he wasn't himself experiencing. Things were always surface level and light and fun, but we never really explored or built an emotional connection between us.

I ignored it at the time, but I wanted to be able to express the deepest parts of me and my partner to do the same. I would envision a relationship where we were able to talk about anything and know that it would always be a safe and supportive space. I would picture us lying in bed at night talking about the littlest things and the biggest things as the early morning hours snuck up on us. Instead, we slept with our backs turned to each other, as I stared off into the blank space in front of me. A spiral of thoughts rotating through my mind. Wondering how I got here once again. I felt so alone, even when he was right there next to me. The type of foundation I was craving didn't exist between us.

As the lonely nights became my new normal, I realized how painfully ashamed of who I was and always felt inferior to him. On the outside he had such a picture-perfect life. He grew up with a well-rounded family and I don't think he ever had to face the level of adversity like I had. I was embarrassed I couldn't say that I came from a similar situation, so I hid a lot of my past from him, only scratching the surface of the truth I had buried so deep within me. I am completely at fault for this, and I was terrified if he knew the real depths of it all, he wouldn't love me anymore. Reminding me that I had been shown this time and time again from the people who should've been able to love me so easily but never could. I thought, "Why would someone so smart and successful want to be with someone so broken?"

Our relationship was built on what wasn't said. Each silence became another brick in a wall between us—my unspoken shame about my past on one side, his emotional unavailability on the other. We were architects of our own isolation, constructing a perfectly presentable life while the foundation crumbled beneath our feet. On paper, we were perfect. In reality, we were two people playing house, neither brave enough to admit we were acting in different plays.

When I reflect back on this time in my life and the tremendous lack of faith I had, I realize how badly I needed to accept God's love at that time. The irony wasn't lost on me that I was seeking salvation in a relationship while running from the very source of true salvation. Each time I chose security over authentic connection, I was really choosing fear over faith. God was offering unconditional love, but I was too busy trying to earn conditional acceptance to notice. My spiritual bankruptcy mirrored my emotional one—both accounts overdrawn from years of trying to find external solutions to internal wounds. I just wanted to be chosen by someone, when in reality, all I needed to see is that God has already chosen me. Instead, I let anger and bitterness sit in my driver's seat and continued down the road thinking God was once again punishing me. So further and further I drifted from Him. I was trying to control everything around me when all I really needed to do was just surrender myself to Him and trust that He was always in control. He should've been the one in the driver's seat. Being in a position of questioning my faith, I wasn't prepared, but it was about to be tested once again.

Chapter Six

Nicole. My sister. A tortured soul that I may never fully comprehend. I previously shared some of the trials she faced when we were growing up. These, however, only scratched the surface of what brewed deep within her.

Nicole carried some of the heavier burdens when it came to our mom because unlike my brother and I, she stayed in contact with our mom throughout most of her life. She had this constant weight holding her down like a ton of bricks. She felt that if she didn't stay in contact with her, we'd never know where Mom was—or if she was alive. I think all three of us often wondered if she was okay or where she was living. My sister couldn't carry the weight of that wonder so she stayed in my mom's life so we always knew where we could find her. She would make sure to tell me every time my mom was evicted and moving to another apartment, whether she was drinking or on one of her many attempts to be sober, or if she and her abusive boyfriend were still together or not. Nicole was the only link our mom had to what was happening in our lives. I never understood at the time why

Nicole tried to keep in contact with her, but she was also a young girl with every hope in her heart that her mom would change.

My mom and sister had a bond that was different from what my brother and I had with her. I always felt growing up that my mom was by far the closest to my sister. I think she saw so much of herself in Nicole, and it connected them in ways only they could understand. They both had very addictive personalities and they bonded over those characteristics in one another. Nicole used to tell me that when she was with my mom, it was some of the only times she didn't feel judged or that she was doing something wrong all the time. Feeling like an outcast to the rest of our family, she felt accepted by our mom.

I was recently looking through some of our childhood photos and I noticed something as I flipped through the faint memories of our childhood. Photos of summers at our aunt's lake cabin swimming with our cousins, Christmas mornings diving into the tower of gifts waiting for us, many birthday cakes with glowing candles matching our ages. Core memories that a child would typically be beaming in the photos—but not her. In almost every photo that my sister was in, she was either not smiling or not making eye contact with the camera. She had this withdrawn demeanor about herself. Closing herself off from any form of human connection, only because she was holding on to the one she needed the most—our mom. The sadness in her eyes could tell you a thousand words. She had these big, beautiful brown eyes that could show even the slightest bit of excitement or the deepest sorrow of pain with one simple look. Either way, when you looked at her, you could almost feel exactly what she was feeling in that very moment. They carried that much conviction.

However, her smile was what most people were drawn to. It was impossible to forget and still the first thing I see when she comes into my memory. I can close my eyes at any moment and see it so clearly. I looked up to her a lot when we were young and would only hope to be as beautiful as she was when I grew up. She had no idea how much beauty she was keeping from the world around her. Not just on the outside, but inside as well. People used to tell us how much we looked alike growing up, and I always thought to myself, "If only I could be a fraction of how pretty she is." We both had dark brown hair, but she got my mom's brown eyes. I was the only one of the three of us that got my dad's hazel eyes with a mix of green, blue, and yellow. Yet, I secretly loved when people would tell us we looked alike, and I took it as a huge compliment. I'm not sure she felt the same level of gratitude being compared to her much younger sister, but I know I always did.

I admired her in so many ways when we were growing up, but things weren't always so good between us. The four-year age gap caused most of our childhood to be filled with us fighting and terrorizing one another. This usually meant me sneaking into her much cooler bedroom, covered in cool posters of teenage heartthrobs scattered around the walls, tons of makeup and hair products that I would've done just about anything to use. I would try her clothes on when she wasn't home and pretend to be just like her. I was that annoying little sister that just wanted to do everything she did. Despite all this, there were times she was my biggest protector.

Even when we were young and at odds, when we'd stay

with our mom, she would let me sleep with her in her bed. She could feel the amount of anxiety that would fill every ounce within me when we were there. There were so many nights, as my mom and her boyfriend were fighting, she would hold me tightly and sing to me. One song in particular was "True Colors" by Cyndi Lauper. It was a song our mom used to sing to her and me when we were little. I would wrap my arms around her and sob as she told me everything was going to be okay. Even if we weren't the closest at that point in our lives, she would've done anything to protect me. A reason I felt at odds between her and our family. She was always there for me when I needed her, and I couldn't turn my back on her when she in turn needed me just as much.

But as our lives evolved and our hearts matured, a connection between us grew so wildly. It was a commitment to one another because our mom wasn't in our lives, so we promised each other we would always be there in not just the big moments of our lives, but even the little ones too.

The biggest shift in that direction happened when my sister was 19 and I was 15. She became pregnant unexpectedly with her boyfriend at that time. He became abusive towards my sister, but luckily she left him when that started. I think when she learned she was pregnant she realized that wasn't the environment she wanted to raise a child in. Knowing firsthand how terrifying it was to watch our own mom be subjected to such terrible abuse. She was determined to raise the baby alone if that was what she had to do. I never doubted her for a second, my sister was made to be a mom.

As the end of her pregnancy neared, I would spend time at her small and modest apartment sorting through all her new baby stuff she had ready. We would go through all the cute little baby outfits that were freshly washed in a baby-scented detergent. She was so organized and seemed so thrilled to be starting her journey in motherhood despite still being somewhat of a child herself. She was always so good at taking care of other people. Throughout high school she worked in an assisted living facility where she worked with adults with disabilities. They absolutely loved and adored my sister. She had this special way of making them feel "normal." She didn't see their disabilities when she was with them. She treated them just like anyone else and I think that's why they grew to love her so much. They felt seen by her. When she went to college, she was going to school to be an early childhood special education teacher. I always knew it took someone special to go into a field like that and it couldn't have been a more perfect fit for her. She had a way of bringing joy to everyone's life around her. Something I don't think she ever realized about herself.

As she was heading to one of her last baby appointments before her due date, I was at my parents' house when my dad got the phone call. It was the hospital calling to let him know that during my sister's appointment, they weren't able to find the baby's heartbeat. She was in such a state of shock she couldn't get herself to make the phone call herself. She had to have the doctor call because she couldn't even speak. She was just one week away from her due date. One week. That's when they told her she would have to give birth naturally to the baby due to her being so far along in her pregnancy.

The next week was a complete blur. I don't think my sister got out of bed that entire week. She just laid there with her hand on her stomach. Almost as if she was hoping to feel a sudden kick or movement from the baby. One that would wake her up from the nightmare she was living. To say she was devastated was an understatement. As she got admitted to the hospital, I knew that I couldn't leave her side so our grandma, aunt, cousin, and I spent days in the hospital with her while they induced her into labor.

After two long and grueling days of labor, the baby was born. You could feel the immediate sadness fill the room. The sound of silence was deafening. All you could hear were the monitors faintly beeping in the background. The smell of sterile equipment overpowering us. It felt so cold and dark in the room. When it should have been filled with the first cries of a newborn baby. You could feel every bit of sorrow she was feeling. She just held that baby for what seemed like hours and stared with complete adoration for him. I was only 15 at the time and didn't know what to do in a situation like this. I felt so inadequate to carry something so heavy. I didn't have the right words or actions to give her in that moment that I know she needed, I felt like there was nothing I could say that would take the pain away that she was feeling. At one point she looked up at me with those beautiful brown eyes that were filled with utter sadness and said to me, "I can't believe how much he looks like you." That one sentence almost broke me. I couldn't hold it together. I sat down next to her and held her for as long as I could. Tears dripping down my neck, snot seeping from my nose. I realized she didn't need me to say the right thing to her in that moment, she just needed me. Just like when we were younger and she would hold me for as long as I needed. So that's what I did. I held her as she held her baby and we sat in what felt like the darkest room in the world at that exact moment in time.

As you could imagine, this ended up being a significant turning point in her life. She blamed herself for losing the baby even though the doctors assured her it was nothing that she did. She replayed those last weeks of her pregnancy over and over again in her head trying to figure out what she had done wrong. She silently tortured herself, and I don't think she was ever the same again. I think one of the hardest parts of it all is that the doctors couldn't give her any answers. They had no idea what caused this to happen, and she tried her best to move forward but this loss and the guilt that came with it was something that she would carry with her for the rest of her life. That light and spark in her eyes never came back after that. Similar to my mom, her eyes became empty and sad. Feeling like I was locking eyes with a complete stranger at times.

As the years followed, my sister ended up developing an unhealthy relationship with alcohol, similar to our mom. She drank a lot in college and had multiple DUIs while she was there. She was becoming quite reckless when she would drink and, like myself, was sabotaging any relationship she was in. She was more broken than I was, but I didn't realize how bad her relationship with alcohol was until I lived with her after I graduated college.

We were so excited to start this phase of our life together. It didn't take me long after moving in to realize how dark things were with her drinking. There were so many times I would come home from my retail management job late in the evenings wondering what state I would find her in. Would she be sober and her typical bubbly self? Would she be a bottle of vodka deep and passed out in her bed? I never knew what I was walking into, but I braced myself every single day never knowing what I would find. I would savor the times when she was smiling and happy as I walked through the door. Waiting for me to cook dinner together, turn on one of our favorite rom com movies and sit together on the couch until late into the night. After going through my mom's journey with alcohol, I knew these moments with her were going to be minimal, so I took any opportunity to share in her happiness with her. Hearing her laugh and seeing her smile.

Things as simple as going to the grocery store together were some of the most fun times I had with her while we lived together. We would slowly walk down every aisle and plan our entire week of meals that we would make together. Oftentimes we talked about our favorite foods our dad cooked for us growing up and tried to replicate some of his best recipes. I would be hopeful for the days ahead and then I'd be hit with the sudden harsh reality that she was living two very different lives. And I'd come home the next day to the sister who would cry herself to sleep, accompanied by a bottle of alcohol.

She was drinking to numb any pain she was feeling. Like the many masks I would wear, this was hers. Every problem of hers she felt could be drowned away with alcohol. Followed by hours of crying at night until she passed out. Recounting every mistake she made throughout her life. It was so difficult to watch. What started as a few drinks started to build to more. She would consume an entire bottle of alcohol in one day if I was gone. She was a ticking time bomb. As I would return home from work at night, I would have to help guide her up the stairs to put her to bed as she would put on a balancing act like she was fine. I lost count of the times I would have to help her shower, get her pajamas on, and brush her teeth for her. Basic things she was incapable of doing for herself because she was so belligerent. I was hiding all this from the world around us because I felt if I said anything I would be betraying her.

It got so bad that I started preparing myself that I might walk in and find her dead one day. There were a few times I would get home from work late into the night. I would slowly open the door to her bedroom and find her sprawled across her bed with a bottle within arm's reach. I would shake her over and over until she would slightly wake up. I would have this faint wave of panic set in thinking I wasn't going to be able to get her up. I played through this scenario in my head so many times prepping myself for what I would do. I felt like I was the only person in her life that knew how bad things were getting but didn't know what to do or who to tell. She would beg me when she was drinking to not say anything to anyone about it. I felt obligated to protect her in some way because she already had so many issues with our family, I knew she didn't need another reason for them all to hate her. So, I kept quiet and just hoped for the best that she would figure it out at some point. We would argue a lot and I thought if she could feel how angry it made me, it would be enough to get her to stop. That she would suddenly snap out of it and realize what she was doing to herself.

This started to cause a huge wedge in our relationship though. Watching her almost drink herself to death every night was so triggering for me, as it reminded me of the nights I would spend watching my mom do the same thing. I had taken a completely different path with alcohol at this point in my life and just couldn't understand how she could be doing this to herself after going through everything we did with our mom. It was like I was living with two different people. Sober Nicole. Drunk Nicole. They weren't the same. Sober Nicole would snap back into her typical and normal self, acting like the previous night's events never happened. I think ignoring the situation made her feel like it wasn't true. That she didn't have a problem.

When I moved out of my sister's house into the house I bought with my husband, I felt somewhat relieved honestly. The weight of her drinking and trying to navigate that all alone was starting to really wear on me. Right before I moved out, she had met someone and they were getting really serious. I was so happy that she had found someone who seemed to truly love her and made her so happy. I thought maybe this relationship would change her, and when they got engaged, I was so thrilled thinking some of the pain she had been holding onto would hopefully disappear.

As wedding planning started to take place, I began to notice that their relationship maybe wasn't so picture perfect after all. I would get phone calls from her telling me about another huge fight that they had. My sister struggled with trust and abandonment issues, and she was constantly accusing him of cheating or doing something else behind her back. It would get even worse when they were drinking together. I started to grow concerned when we were only about 7 months out from their wedding and I felt like they didn't have anything planned yet. She kind of kept pushing things off whenever we would talk about it, and I almost felt like she knew the wedding wasn't going to happen. And then one phone call in particular confirmed that all my worries were true.

Her fiancé was gone for the weekend, and she called me hysterical saying he was with a bunch of guy friends and she thought he was cheating on her. They were fighting over the phone all weekend, but I could tell that she wasn't in a great head space when I talked to her. I was so frustrated that this was happening once again to the point where I had to call our cousin, who we were both close with, to drive over to her house and check on her. Luckily, she got her in bed and she was fine, but we both grew worried when we saw just how bad things were getting with her.

When I would see her, it would look like she hadn't slept in days with dark circles under her eyes. Her frame shrinking before my very eyes. She looked so frail and tired. I felt a tremendous amount of guilt feeling like she was going to do something she would regret so, I decided to call my dad and tell him what was going on. When I told my dad the situation, I think it was so hard for him to believe at that time because he hadn't been living with her and witnessing it for himself. He said, "Well if that's what she wants to do and how she's going to live her life that's her choice." I think he truly didn't realize just how bad it was. And then a few short weeks later, our lives changed forever.

It was a Saturday morning, and I was traveling back to my hometown to spend the day watching my nephew's basketball tournament and spend some time with my family. While I was at one of his games I was talking to my sister-in-law and told her what had been going on. I vividly remember standing in the doorway to the gym and her and I discussing everything. I looked right at her while the loud sounds of basketballs being dribbled filled the air and the loud buzzers of the timeclocks going off and said, "I think she is going to do something stupid. I just have this feeling." I will never forget the moment my phone rang that night when I was back at my own house. It was my dad, and he told me the words I will never forget: "Nicole died. She killed herself." His voice filled with pure devastation that he could barely even say the words. And as sad as it is, all I could think in the moments that followed was, "I knew this was going to happen." I feel like in some ways I had been preparing myself for this moment for years.

As we prepared for her funeral I would have so many members of our family and friends continue to ask me so many questions. They were all struggling with this sudden news. Most of them not knowing the depths of her struggles. They would applaud me for my strength as we managed through those first few days trying to make sense of it all. I took a sense of pride when anyone would say this to me. I wanted to prove to them that this wasn't another thing that would break me. That I was strong enough to handle anything that came my way. When inside I was doing every-thing and anything I could to hold myself together. I was so angry at her. The promises we once made that we would always be there for one another were suddenly gone. And yet again I had someone who I loved more than anything leave me. My head was so clouded with this thought process that for years I ignored the fact that she was struggling so much too. To the point where ending her life felt like her only option to escape the pain she was feeling.

Her funeral would be the last time I ever saw my mom. One of my mom's sisters called me and asked how I would feel if they brought her to the funeral. I said of course I would be okay with her attending, it was her daughter after all. I just had one request from them, I asked them to tell her I had no interest in speaking with her and to give me my space. It had been about 10 years since I had seen her, and I knew if she saw me she would immediately come up to me and try and mend our relationship. I knew she was still not sober, so I didn't want to put myself through that all over again. Especially when I was in the midst of losing the one person I was closest to in the world for that very same reason.

When my mom arrived at her visitation, it didn't take her more than one second before running up to me and pulling me in for a hug. I could smell the alcohol from the night before escaping from every pore. A smell I had become all too familiar with. She promised she wouldn't talk to me and of course she couldn't respect my request. Once again it was all about her. I had to push her off of me and say to her, "Please don't touch me or talk to me. You are here to mourn the death of your daughter, not pretend you have one who is still part of your life." I don't even know how those words came out of my mouth. I'm not a cruel person and I know that wasn't the best thing to say in that moment as we were all grieving a huge loss, including her. But I was so angry. She never once thought she did anything wrong or how much she had hurt us all and her lack of accountability for the trauma she caused us made me want to scream. I hadn't dealt with all that yet and had been pushing it all further down in the depths of myself and avoiding it. I just wasn't ready to face it. I had no idea that would be the last time I would ever see my mom. And honestly, it's sad to think about it now. That the last moments with her were spent at my sister's funeral.

I carried my sister's death with me everywhere. Like a weighted vest I could never take off. Every step, I could feel the hole of her absence. I still can't get through an entire day without thinking about her. And I think this will always be the case. However, instead of being angry when I think of her, like I spent those first 10 years after her death doing, I now have an immense amount of gratitude for the 25 years I did have with her. I will cherish the time she was in my life and a lot of the things I do today I do for her. The things she never got a chance to do herself.

It makes me sad she never got to see me get married, be there when my kids were born who I know she would've loved like they were her own. I'm sad they won't ever get to meet her. She is often someone I pray about, who I talk to when I'm having a hard day. She knows the most intimate thoughts in my mind and my deepest desires. I find peace in her existence and can feel her all around me. Even though her death pulled me even further from God at the time, she's a huge reason why I've reconnected with my faith now. To know that God's love is all we truly need and how much that has saved me. I wish she would've known that and sought him in those final moments of her struggles. I believe in my heart she would still be here today if that were the case. Losing her made me realize how fragile life is and it deepened my commitment to healing.

Chapter Seven

The pregnancy test trembled in my hands, two pink lines appearing like a miracle after eighteen months of negative results and fertility treatments. Tears blurred my vision—tears of joy mingled with unexpected fear. This moment I'd dreamed about my entire life was finally here, yet I couldn't shake the whisper of doubt beneath my racing heart. "What if I become like her?" The question I'd been running from since childhood surfaced in the harsh glare of the bathroom light. After all the doctor's appointments, the procedures, the disappointments, and now this sudden joy, I realized the hardest journey was just beginning—the one where I'd have to face the mother I feared becoming.

Motherhood—something I dreamt about my entire life. I had this vision of what type of mom I would be someday. Loving, involved, nurturing, gentle, intentional, admirable. I often imagined the kind of mom I wanted to be—the one I never had. In every disappointing scenario I went through with my mom, I would envision how I would handle it if I were the mom. But becoming a mom was once again going to present me with another difficult roadblock.

About a year after we got married, my husband and I decided we wanted to try to start a family. Naïvely, I thought we'd conceive within a month or two, and we would be staring at a positive pregnancy test. God had other plans for us though. Considering our already unstable foundation of a relationship, we were about to have even more stacked against us—walls so high we couldn't see a way out.

The first few months of trying went by and nothing. Although I wasn't too concerned yet, the disappointment began to build as each month went by producing another negative pregnancy test. Each time we approached another test, our hearts filled with hope. But that hope would just as quickly disappear when the reality set in. It stopped feeling hopeful and started feeling like a chore wrapped in disappointment. Fast forward to when we were just shy of a year of trying and still nothing, I figured it was time to check in with my doctor and see what we could do. I remember going to that first appointment, filled with anxiety not quite knowing what to expect. I could feel the fear and doubt take over as they asked us question after question trying to understand our circumstances. When my doctor came in, it was the only moment during that entire appointment I felt relief. She sat down, put her hands on my knees with the most endearing look in her eyes, she said, "We will find a way to get you that baby I know you are just dying to meet one day." Tears fell from my eyes, and it felt like it was the first breath I took since I got there.

My doctor advised us to run a bunch of fertility tests on the both of us and when the results surprisingly looked normal, I was left feeling even more confused. Although thrilled to get good news like that, it left us with more questions than answers. So, if everything looked normal, why wasn't I getting pregnant?

With the guidance of my doctor, we decided we would try to start the first phase of fertility treatments. And month after month we were still hit with one negative pregnancy test after another. Every doctor's appointment would come to check on each cycle's progress, and I would sit in my car beforehand and barely muster up enough energy to walk through those doors once again. I'd stare at the ultrasound monitor and would instantly know it was another failed round. The doctor would tell me she was sorry and I'd force a smile across my face and say, "That's okay, next month will be the month." She'd leave the room and I'd just sit there alone and cry before pulling myself together enough to walk through the lobby filled with pregnant women waddling with glee for their upcoming babies arrivals. Because the appointments were so often, I would go alone most of the time. I would have to make the dreaded phone call or text to my husband telling him once again it didn't work. I became numb to it all, feeling almost nothing. What started as an exciting journey to starting a family, became a daunting task to complete.

We got to the last and final resort before having to consider IVF. We were about 18 months in, and it was clearly starting to wear on our relationship. The littlest things we would fight over both being on the edge of breaking. The cracks that were crafted through our relationship were cut deeper and deeper as the months went by. It got to the point where we had to consider that maybe having kids wasn't in the plans for us. I was ready to give up. I couldn't help but blame myself thinking it was something I was doing or that something was wrong with me. I would think to myself, of course God isn't allowing you to get pregnant. It's something you've been dreaming of your whole life, and he didn't want me to be happy. He wanted me to suffer even more than I already was. That is truly what I thought and felt. I spent most of my life feeling like he was punishing me over and over and I was at my breaking point to say the least. As we entered that last month of trying, my husband and I had one of the worst fights of our relationship.

We were at my coworkers wedding, and I think we were both so stressed out about trying to get pregnant. We started to take it out on each other and things boiled over that night. The night was filled with drinking and dancing to distract us from our harsh reality we were actually living, but as the night came it turned into one of the worst nights in our relationship. Everyone had been drinking a bit too much and my husband ended up saying something extremely rude to one of my coworkers that was also at the wedding. She was understandably upset and started telling our other coworkers and friends that were there what had happened. Because these were people I worked with, I got so upset that he would cross a line like that.

I hated who he became when he drank. He was sloppy and outspoken. Deep down I wanted the husband who was fun to be around when we would have a night out. Instead, I was bracing myself for impact. Wondering what he would say to offend someone we were with. Furious, I went to go back to our hotel room, and he saw how upset I was as I stormed through the hotel lobby where the after party was starting. He ran after me and asked me what was wrong. I turned to him with fire blasting through my veins and yelled and told him how embarrassed I was. That I had to face these people on Monday, and it didn't look good that I was the girl with the husband who runs his mouth when he drinks. This immediately set him off and he got so angry at me, he started yelling and tried to run away from me back to our room. I ran after him because once again I was to blame for what happened. He didn't want to take accountability for what he did, so instead blamed me for my reaction. He shoved me as I tried to get back into our hotel room. Then he slammed the door in my face. A few people even came out of their rooms to check what all the commotion was about and saw what happened. I just brushed it off and smiled and told them everything was okay. I felt the shame building more layers as I lied to complete strangers about what had just happened. How did something my husband do and say turn into my fault? Now I was the one left feeling that I did something wrong.

I stayed in a friends room for the night to let us both cool off. That morning when we had to make the silent and dreaded long drive home, he said the words I never thought I'd hear come out of his mouth. He said, "I want a divorce, we will split everything evenly and just go our separate ways." Every inch of my body felt like it was in a knot when I heard him speak the words I've been terrified to hear. This was the first of many threats that I would get over the course of the next couple years. I was devastated and begged him not to leave me. The same way I would beg my mom and sister to stop drinking. I couldn't imagine being alone, I was utterly terrified. Deep down I felt like he knew how scared I was for people to leave me that if he threatened it enough, he knew I would do whatever it took to get him to stay. Looking back, I think this would've been the best time to get out of the marriage. But I was so broken still that I did everything I could to keep us held together. And then one month after this, I got the positive pregnancy test we had been waiting for. I knew right in that moment I had to try and make things work.

This wave of good news swept all the negative right under the rug. It was the perfect distraction to the glaring problems we were facing. It felt like we could finally take a breath. There was a small part of me thinking that this baby would change everything for us. That suddenly all our problems would go away just like that. Every ounce of doubt about my marriage that was lingering became covered by the blessing we were just given. I was finally going to be a mom and that's all I could think about.

The few days of waiting for my first ultrasound felt like months. But the day was finally here where I would get to see the little baby growing inside of me. After the long journey of trying to get pregnant, I was just hoping we weren't going to be faced with any more bad news. I just wanted to know the baby was growing and healthy. I felt confident since my symptoms came quickly and fierce. I was already spending most of my day in the bathroom throwing up, but I took it as a good sign things were progressing the way they should. Little did I know, the intense symptoms I was feeling was because there wasn't just one baby growing inside of me—there were two. When the words, "It's twins," came out of my doctor's mouth, my husband and I just sat there shocked. Neither one of us could speak. We knew there were chances of this based on our fertility treatments, but you never think it's going to actually happen to you. My husband, although slightly panicked, was able to give a nervous smile while the doctor shared the news. A wave of fear came flooding through me. I was mixed with excitement that I was being gifted two babies to love, coupled with fear of the unknown. Could our marriage handle what we were about to take on? I knew we were both capable of being great parents, but would this pull us further apart as husband and wife? Time would tell but my goal and purpose was to make sure I got those babies here safely and healthy. That's all that mattered in that moment.

My dream of becoming a mom was finally about to come true. But I would've never expected things to be the way they were once they were here. My pregnancy was tough, and it took a major toll on my body carrying two beautiful and healthy babies. But I don't think I was quite prepared for the events after they were born. They were premature, which was to be expected, and overall healthy with a few little complications the first 24 hours. After that though, I just didn't feel like I was bonding with them the way I expected. My body was having a hard time producing milk due to having a cesarean and them being five weeks early. I was doing everything I could to try to improve my milk supply, but nothing was working. While the boys were in the NICU, I would sit between feedings and do power pumps. I was beyond exhausted trying to make it work. All the while my husband was putting what felt like a ton of pressure on me and would make comments about how expensive formula was going to be for two growing babies. I felt like it was my job to be able to feed them and once again I felt like I wasn't good enough. I couldn't even breastfeed my own babies and I didn't realize how much that issue was preventing me from having the bonding experience I wanted so badly with my children.

I pictured myself being this calm and nurturing mother, but instead I was hardened by the harsh realities I was facing. I struggled with the baby blues those first couple weeks after they were born and couldn't express the level of anxiety I was feeling about every single simple decision I had to make throughout the day. Every conversation with the nurses and doctors overwhelmed me. I felt like I had no idea what I was doing. I started to overthink everything and questioned my capabilities to be a mom.

The anxiety was suffocating—I'd wake up drenched in sweat, my mind racing with fears of failure. I would spend my time during the middle of the night feedings feeling like maybe I wasn't actually meant to be a mom. I'd look down at these beautiful babies and tell myself they deserved more than me. I would cry as I'd tell them how sorry I was for failing them. I suffered alone and would convince myself they were better off without me. I was putting so much pressure on myself to be perfect; I was crumbling before my very eyes and still couldn't see it. As I'd stare into the darkness of the night, I would question my abilities as a mom. I'd wonder if it was because I didn't have a strong relationship with my own mom that I just didn't know how to be one myself? I was never shown unconditional love by my mom, so was I inadequate to care for my own children?

I now know that my thoughts and feelings weren't normal to be having as a first time mom and it got to the point where it was almost debilitating. Everything stressed me out, from feeding and sleep schedules, fussy babies, diaper changes, everything. The sweet moments of babies cooing, giggles flowing, and huge gummy smiles as I walked into their room every morning were overshadowed with the immense amount of anxiety I was feeling. I had a really hard time letting go of anyone else caring for the kids other than me. If they didn't stick to our strict schedule everything would be thrown off and I'd be the one to have to suffer. I wanted full control of everything, and it was depleting everything I had. The deafening silence of my struggles was like a weight I carried with me everywhere that only I could feel but no one else could see. It was the most isolated and alone I had ever felt in my entire life. The mask of shame I wore most of my life was quickly back on, and I couldn't get the words out to say I needed help.

One other thing I didn't expect after becoming a mom was how much anger would brew within me. Holding my babies, I suddenly remembered my mom leaving me in the car. Tears blurred my vision as I hugged my children even tighter. Here I had children of my own now and I couldn't fathom putting them through what my mom put me and my siblings through. I wasn't expecting motherhood to be so triggering for me, and I wasn't ready to face all of that on top of dealing with a major bout of postpartum anxiety. I felt like I had no one to turn to in that moment. Here I had spent years wanting to have children of my own, so I felt selfish for complaining about how I was feeling. I told myself to just get over it and try and move forward. But that's not how trauma works. You can't just bury it deep down inside of you and expect it to just go away. It just ends up spilling over into every aspect of your life. I was too proud to say out loud that I was struggling. I didn't feel like I had a husband who understood what I was feeling, and I felt so much shame in it all.

I feel like this was the point that I completely lost myself. I was just going through the motions, carrying all the mental load when it came to keeping a family running. My husband would make snide comments about my rigid routines with the kids, but little did he know it was the only way I felt I could survive. I was drowning in motherhood and felt like I had no one who could help keep me above water. I now hate that my kids had that for their mom those first important years of their lives. And I wish I would've recognized that earlier and got the help I really needed.

As the twins got a bit older, things started to seem more manageable for myself. We had the discussion a few times about whether or not we would try to have another baby, but we were both ignoring the red flags of our relationship. When my twins were just two, my husband and I had another huge fight at our friend's wedding. But once again it ended up in him saying we should just get divorced. I was a complete mess. Here I was struggling so much on the inside, I had two young kids in the thick of their toddler years and being a single mom was something that terrified me. I told myself to do whatever you have to do to make this work. So, I begged him once again not to leave me. I told him I'd change and do everything he needed me to. When you already feel poorly about yourself and something like this happens, the amount of guilt and shame you feel is indescribable. Our arguments always felt like this to me—I was always the one who was wrong, I had to be the one to apologize and compromise my needs or beliefs to keep him happy. I never felt that I was met with empathy, understanding, patience, or consideration. Everything was my fault. Period. I realized bringing another child into this mess probably wasn't going to help things and we finally agreed we were both okay being done having kids. After all, we had such a hard time getting pregnant with our twins, I think we both weren't ready to sign up for another long journey of trying to get pregnant again. Certainly, we both knew our marriage wouldn't survive that now that we were already parents to twins. And then bam, out of nowhere, I found out I was pregnant once again.

I don't want to sound like I wasn't happy about having our third child. I wanted the best for my kids, and I felt like we were bringing another child into a messy situation. I wasn't being the best mom already, so how could I possibly care for another baby? I felt so much guilt already for not being the mom I always thought I would be.

I was at work when I found out. I had been having a tough couple of weeks and was unusually emotional about things that typically wouldn't bother me. A close friend of mine that I worked with pulled me aside one day and asked if I was maybe pregnant. I laughed it off and said there is no possible way. Later that day she dropped by my desk and brought me a pregnancy test. She felt so strongly this was the case that she was insistent that I take a test. So confident that I wasn't, I walked into the bathroom and took the test. As the minutes passed, my mind started to spin. I said to myself, "You can't possibly be pregnant right?" I sat there pacing the tiny stall convincing myself there wasn't any way.

As I looked down and saw it was positive, I was in complete shock. Within a few seconds the tears started to form. I couldn't believe this was happening. One of my first thoughts when I saw the positive pregnancy test was, why would you bring another child into this mess? Instead of thinking about all the joy this precious human would bring to my life, all I could think about was how much stress it was about to put on my already rocky marriage.

Overwhelmed by this news, I walked to my desk and told my coworker to meet me by the elevators so we could go for a walk. I was shaking as we entered the elevator together just trying to hold it together until we weren't around anyone else. As we walked through the skyways of the hustle and bustle of downtown, everything around me became a blur. I shared my fears of having another baby. I cried as I went through all the scenarios in my head that was spinning. Will I be able to give more love to another child? Will I fail after this pregnancy too? Will my marriage survive the stress? We talked about how I was going to tell my husband. I needed to pull myself together so I could go home and tell him the news. I wasn't quite sure how he was going to react. I thought maybe he'll feel disappointed too?

As I walked in the door after work, I saw him at the kitchen table with the twins. I set my bag down and walked over to him. I hesitated for a moment and finally mustered up the courage to say, "I'm pregnant." I was shocked when a huge smile fell across his face. I wasn't expecting this reaction from him. Wasn't he feeling the pressures we were already under? Why couldn't I feel that way when I found out? I felt like the worst mom in the world after that. How could I be sad about bringing another life into this world? I didn't realize this at the time, but I wasn't so sad about having another child. It was more so feeling that I wasn't bringing this child into the best environment possible. I wanted to give my kids everything and I already felt like a failure, how could I be a better mom having even more on my plate?

Now that my youngest is here, it's without question he was the missing puzzle piece that I had no idea we were missing. I was so scared that this would drive us even further apart, adding the stress of another person to care for, going through a hard pregnancy again. But sometimes you don't know you need something until it's placed in your life. Having my third child was all of this and more for me. He's been one of my greatest blessings and has taught me more about myself than I will ever be able to teach him. He is the child I wish I could've been more like when I was a younger. He's funny, outgoing, feels every emotion unapologetically, and has so much confidence in who he is. It most certainly was part of God's plan, and I can't imagine our lives without those three beautiful boys now. It was all meant to be.

Although my journey through motherhood wasn't what I envisioned, it's unlocked a part of me I didn't know was there. It's forced me to face some of my darkest and deepest trauma. It was everything I didn't know I needed. My three amazing boys completely saved me. I'm not perfect by any means, but I now know that I was meant to be their mom. Every time I look into my children's eyes, I remind myself that I can't let my past define their future. Every day I commit to working towards a better version of myself for them. They will always be my driving force and every step we've taken to get where we are today was worth it. Even in some of my darkest days, they were the light I needed to keep me going.

I want them to know how much they have changed me; in all the ways I needed. Everything I do to better myself, is in service to them. They deserve a love from me that I was never gifted from my own mom. It's a promise I made to myself that I would give my children all the love they deserve and so much more. They are my greatest teachers, and every prayer answered. I will spend my entire life loving them fiercely. Thank you, boys, for giving me the greatest gift one could ever receive. I will love you all until my heart stops.

Chapter Eight

A fter years of silence, waves of emotions would flood me as a new mom. I would think about my own mom often and wonder if she ever got sober. I wondered if she knew I had kids of my own. But I never looked for her because I didn't want to introduce her back into my life now that I had children to protect. I didn't want to set them up for the disappointment I felt from her as a child. Secretly there was always a small part of me that hoped I would hear from her one day, calling me to tell me she finally quit drinking and that she was doing well. That maybe we could mend our relationship to some degree. Part of me wanted her to see the life that I had without her. It was as if I almost just wanted to say to her, "See, you didn't end up ruining me after all." I would've been lying to myself and everyone around me if I had said that out loud though. Those unhealed fragments of me were about to be exposed to the world as my future of reestablishing a relationship with my mom came crashing down.

It was June of 2021, and I had just gotten home from

work and my husband was on his way home with the kids. I was starting to get dinner ready, and my phone rang. It wasn't a number I recognized so I let it go to voicemail. When I heard the ping that I had a voicemail I decided to listen to it quickly. It was the Stearns County Sheriff's department, and the officer was trying to get in contact with me. He left a number for me to call back and said that it was urgent. I knew right in that moment that it was about my mom. That was the county she lived in most of her life, and I assumed that was still the area she was living in at the time. This was the phone call I had been bracing myself for. It was like I had been holding my breath for fifteen years waiting for this exact moment to happen. Hesitant, I called him back and before he would share any information, he asked me a few questions to verify who I was. The child inside me was screaming to just tell me what was going on, desperate to know just any morsel of information about my mom. But the adult version of me was hoping time would halt to stop the news I knew was about to crush me.

At one point I remember he asked for my address and at first I didn't want to share it with him until I knew what he was contacting me about. I mean I assumed it was about my mom, but part of me didn't know if maybe she was still alive and just in trouble, needing someone to bail her out of jail again. I didn't want her to have any of my personal information in case she would use it to find me. I told him where I was coming from and he understood, and then he finally said the words I had been bracing myself for. "Well, I don't know how to tell you this, but we received a call to do a welfare check on your mom and we found her deceased in her apartment." Even though I had been anticipating this phone call for most of my life, you can still never prepare yourself for that moment. It brought me right back to the night my dad called to tell me my sister had died. So many thoughts flood your mind in that single moment. My thoughts were all over the place going from "Did that boyfriend of hers actually go through with killing her?" to "Now I'll never get a chance to have any type of relationship with her ever again" and "Was she sober when she died?" So many questions flooded my mind.

Then the officer asked me a question I wasn't remotely prepared for. He said, "Well, since you and your brother Josh are her next of kin, we need you to tell us where you want us to take her body." I was so taken aback by this. Filled with disbelief that a decision that carried so much weight was about to be placed on my shoulders. I couldn't help but think to myself that she was practically a stranger to me. I had no idea what I should do, so I asked him what the options were and he basically said either call a funeral home to start making arrangements and they will take custody of the body or you can release her body to the state and they will take it from there. Although our relationship was strained, the second option just felt so cold to me. How could I just give her away like that and never know where she is laid to rest? I immediately called my brother to talk to him about it. We agreed we needed to figure something out but we both were not prepared to take on the task we were about to face.

The next few weeks were spent going through her tiny apartment trying to figure out what to do with all her stuff. My mom had eclectic taste. Every drawer, every corner, every shelf was covered in some type of item or décor. She would go to thrift stores and buy some of the most ridiculous things and my brother and I were left to sort through every last piece of it. I would find small glass trinkets of red roses—

her favorite flower, wind chimes hanging from every corner of the ceiling, clay bowls filled with jewelry that had tarnished. It was like she was never gone. I could picture her sitting on her worn-out couch surrounded by her dust covered clutter as she carefully combed through her morning paper. The light filtering through the stained-glass window ornaments she carefully hung and I'm sure admired when she'd look at them. Every item we went through had a story. A history of where it had belonged long before it was here with her in her small apartment. I could envision her wandering the nearest thrift shop with a slight smile on her face. Carefully studying all the new items that had come since the last time she was there. Her eyes lighting up when she'd find the perfect item to add to her collection.

There was one item in particular I was hoping I'd stumble upon. When I was younger, she got a ring that had all three of our birthstones, it wasn't my favorite jewelry item of hers, but she loved it more than any other piece she wore. It was something that always reminded me of her. The mom I had before she left. The mom that wore this ring so proudly as she shared the love she had for her three kids. It was the only thing I was planning to keep of hers if I found it. Even though I knew she more than likely lost it along the way, I was hoping she held on to it as a reminder of the three of us. I never found the ring, but I think about it a lot still to this day. Wondering if I would stumble upon it at one of the thrift stores she visited regularly. Or maybe she pawned it years ago to get some cash for her next bottle of liquor. Either way, there is a story behind that ring. One that has so much meaning.

Luckily, and surprisingly, she had left us her final wishes, almost as if she was preparing for her death for a while. She had them written on a recipe card tossed amongst a pile spread across her kitchen table—like a grocery list. She had many health issues over the years, contracting hepatitis at one point, and with her prolonged alcohol use, her health wasn't in the best place. She had even taken the time to take out a small life insurance policy for my brother and me to handle her arrangements. Honestly, I was shocked. The mom I knew was too selfish to realize the burden it would leave my brother and me in, so I was so surprised to find out she had taken the time to leave us with anything. Wanting to honor her wishes, my brother and I worked through detail after detail to determine what we felt was best for her. We visited a few cemeteries and found one we knew she would feel so at peace. Every inch of it was covered in old, established oak trees towered over the headstones of loved ones no longer here. While birds flew from branch to branch with their subtle chirping that you could hear from afar. I sat in the middle of it with my eyes closed, picturing her black, wavy hair flowing freely in the wind. While the sun touched her freckle covered skin as she took in the peaceful moment I was in. It felt so right. My brother and I looked at each other and said, "this is the place she needs to be."

Every other decision the two of us were faced with was determined through so much love and care, despite the pain we both were holding on to. Even though this was one of the most difficult experiences to go through, it brought my brother and me closer. He stayed strong through every step knowing how much I was struggling on the inside. Guiding me the way an older brother does when faced with familial dismay. Between what felt like hundreds of phone calls, multiple days spent going through her things, making her arrangements one by one—he protected me in every way he knew he could. His wife Michelle is also someone I grew closer to throughout this as she showed up for us in every way over those weeks and months following her death. I think she has seen first-hand the impact our lives and circumstances have had on us, and she has always without a doubt shown up for my brother and me in ways I don't think she will ever truly understand. She is someone who has made me feel so seen, understood, and loved as I've had to face some of these difficult moments throughout my life. I am so grateful for the relationships I have with both of them. I don't know how I would've gone through any of this without either of their love and support.

As our time started to come to a close going through her things, all I could think in the back of my mind was, "please let us find a letter from her." All I had hoped for over the years was for her to finally just apologize for what she put us through. For her to finally take responsibility for her actions that left me in fragments of myself. It was the only thing I knew I needed to find any ounce of peace within all this. But as the days started to go by and we weren't finding anything I started to lose hope. Until one final day, my mom's sister was helping us sort through everything and had offered to handle going through the belongings in Mom's bedroom.

We had been avoiding that space knowing that was where she had passed away. She died in her sleep, but she wasn't found for almost a week after her death. The vision of her lying there would flash in my mind every time I walked past the door. It made me so sad that no one realized she was gone. It took one of her neighbors calling the landlord to say that there were a bunch of newspapers stacked up by her door and there was a foul smell starting to fill the hallways. I couldn't bring myself to step into her room when I knew what had happened in there. The last thoughts she had still lingering amongst her memory. Her final breath still filling the air. It was just too hard.

At one point while my aunt was going through her stuff, she came out of the room holding some papers and she looked at me with tears in her eyes. She said, "Katie, I think you need to read this." As I looked down at the paper, I saw the same handwriting that filled the many birthday cards from past years. The handwriting that covered recipe books in her kitchen, and notes to my sister after she died. But there it was. A letter to my brother and me from our mom. I don't want to share the entirety of the letter, but I do want to share the part that I had been hoping for, the words I had been waiting most of my life for:

"To Josh and Katie,

This is the most important thing I had to do. I know when you get this letter it means I'm not here anymore and I never in my wildest dreams ever thought that you would be out of my life forever. I understand why. I let you guys down so much. Abuse and addiction took a toll on me. For the last 20 years I worked on my failures, but it was just too late to reconcile. I regret that every day and how I was never able to recover and be a part of your lives. I think about you every day and how sorry I was that I couldn't just do the right thing. To not be a part of your lives was devastating and boy I missed the most important things in the world, my children and their children. You'll never know how sorry I am that you had to go through that. Losing Nicole, I'm missing her so much. Never a day goes by that I don't think about all three of you. I pray that you and your families have a good life. I'm sorry about us and I never forgot you and how I failed you so bad. Please forgive me!!! I'm so happy you turned out so well,

I regret never knowing my grandchildren and being the mother and grandmother I so longed to be. Just know I never stopped loving you and thinking about you.

Peace and Love, Mom"

And there they were. The words I had been longing for all my life—I'm sorry. Two simple words that carried more peace than I can even comprehend. Two simple words that could have fixed years of pain and hurt in an instant. Two words that were filled with her deepest sorrow and regret. I could hear her voice as I read every single word so carefully. As tears rolled down my cheeks and neck I came back to reality and realized I hadn't taken a single breath while I read the entire letter. Each word peeling a layer of pain away, all while uncovering new ones I'd have to face. Every emotion possible was racing through me. A surge of anger that was quickly followed with an aching relief. Every second a new feeling emerged, followed by a memory of who she used to be. Her words spoken from a place I hadn't been to in so long. It was a glimpse into the heart of the mom I had been longing to see again. Pouring her heart into her final message to her children. I can see her sitting on her bed, holding the pen carefully as she dragged it across the page. Filling it with ink covered in regret. But also seeing a sense of peace come over her. That she could finally share the despair in her heart. The words she probably held onto for so many years that she knew she'd never get to say out loud to us.

Something I was happy to learn while reading it was that she was sober when she passed away, and also when she wrote us that letter. I found out my aunt had been in contact with her, and she shared a little about our lives with our mom. Which gave me some peace knowing she knew I had children of my own, that I was a good mom and that my brother was doing well with his family too. My heart was also breaking knowing I was never going to get the chance to see her ever again. I was sad that she had been sober for some time and never found the courage to reach out to us. I think she felt things weren't repairable at that point, but I do feel I would've been open to meeting her again and tell her about my life. I struggled a lot after her death coming to terms with that. I remember crying in bed one night as I snuggled with the kids while they watched a show before bed. My husband looked up at me and asked what was wrong. I told him that I was having a hard time coming to terms with her death and his response to me was, "I don't understand why this is so hard for you, you didn't even talk to her all these years." Right then and there I knew that he was never going to understand the pain I had been carrying for most of my life and how it has impacted me as a person.

This was also a moment of clarity for me. Seeing that I had ended a generational cycle for my own kids. Feeling the pain that I was swimming in and that I had given my own kids a chance to never feel what I felt as a child—alone. They could go to sleep each night knowing and feeling loved by their mom. A gift I desperately wanted to give all my life and here I was giving them that in the midst of intense grief and trauma of my own. The young girl inside of me whispering "thank you." For not only being the mom I always deserved for my own kids, but for being what she needed all those years as well. It was healing a heart from my past all while changing the one I had in the present.

Part Three

The Path to Healing

The quiet ache of your absence
Clung to my bones like an old shadow
The stillness surrounds me
But it's not empty
In a space where my sorrow lingered
A new quiet grows
My heart once closed in grief
Slowly opens to something new
Something more tender
Softer than I knew I could hold
I release what I lost
Beneath the weight of silence
And in its place
Find a new pulse that moves forward
Taking the past that is now a part of me
Woven into the fibers of my being

Learning to live with both the sorrow and
    renewal
Of a heart that dares to open again

Chapter Nine

A fter my mom's death, I felt a huge shift in myself. I was finally able to admit that I not only needed help, but I wanted help. I had my annual checkup with my doctor on the horizon and knew I had to say something. When she was running through her typical list of questions, I waited patiently for the one about rating my anxiety in everyday life. My hands were sweating as each question was asked and I could feel the words hanging at the tip of my tongue just waiting to be said—"I'm not okay. I don't feel like I even know who I am anymore." A wave of relief washed over me as I swallowed the lump in my throat. I told her about my postpartum anxiety and how it had escalated since then and how I felt I needed to finally see someone. She looked into my eyes with nothing but empathy and said, "It takes a lot of courage to admit when you are not okay. And I'm here to tell you it's okay to not be okay. You just did a really big thing and you should be proud of that." The tears came flowing out of me in that moment. She was so right. This was the first time in my entire life I'd spoken those words. This was a huge step for me.

She immediately gave me a referral and before I knew it, I was back at home scrolling the website, looking through all the therapists. This was during the tail end of covid so most of the therapists were offering virtual sessions only. I was slightly disappointed thinking I would have a hard time connecting with someone in a virtual setting versus in person. To be honest, a lot of the therapists that stood out to me weren't taking any new patients. So I sorted through the handful left that would take new patients and narrowed it down to one. It took me over a week to finally make the phone call to set up my first appointment. I was so scared to start. I honestly felt like I was such a broken mess that no therapist was going to want to help someone like me. But I finally called and made that first appointment.

Before the session, I felt slightly guarded. I had so many thoughts in my mind of what I would want to talk about, but I had no idea where to start. I didn't want to cry or show that I was struggling. I had to constantly remind myself that it was the actual reason why I was there. For the first time in my life, I had to take off all the masks I had been wearing and let her see the real me. And it was terrifying. I felt exposed in a way, just out there with everything in the open. All the things I spent my life burying, were making their way to the surface.

It took me quite a few sessions to get comfortable, and I would say I was pretty resistant to any recommendations my therapist gave me at first. My stomach would be in knots for days leading up to those first few appointments. I would watch the clock closely the day of and think about how I couldn't wait until it would be over. As I sat there in the virtual waiting room, I'd consider leaving the call before it even started—every single time. There was so much anxiety looming over every session it was almost debilitating. Going into it right away, I had the attitude that everything was going to be solved through our sessions only and I didn't have to put any work in beyond that. I couldn't have been more wrong. Talking to someone for one hour every week wasn't going to solve the deep-rooted issues I had been burying myself under for my entire life. I was about to have to put in a ton of work and although I knew I needed to do this, I hadn't prepared myself for just how much work that was going to be.

My therapist would typically try to end each one of our sessions with some homework for myself. Whether it was breathwork, meditation, journaling, prayer. Most of the time I didn't want to do it, or I'd try something once and hate it and would give up after the first try. One thing she was very persistent about was having me do some writing, and it was the absolute last thing I wanted to do. I think she started to realize it was going to take some time to break down the walls I had spent most of my life building around me. A maze full of unexpected turns and roadblocks that were carefully crafted throughout my entire life. And then one day she asked me to write a few letters before our next session. At first I questioned it but I had no idea how eye opening the exercise would be. She gave me three specific people she wanted me to write letters to—my dad, my mom, and my stepmom. At first, I was surprised by one of the names she said, trying to understand how this person stood out to her enough to recommend this, but I went along with it and sat down to start writing.

When I tell you this was a complete turning point in my

healing journey, I wholeheartedly mean it. I couldn't believe what came pouring out of me as I wrote those letters. Things came up that I had never realized affected me the way they did. When I sat down to write the first letter to my dad, I envisioned myself writing about how it was his fault for a lot of what happened throughout my life. I was so surprised when I finished. From what started off as a stiff and angry tone, quickly transpired into a place of understanding, forgiveness, and gratitude. Writing to him, I said: "I didn't know it at the time, but you saved me." It was the first time I reflected on my relationship with my dad realizing how much he sacrificed for my siblings and I. How he, too, was broken and trying his best, giving us everything he could at that time. I never once felt that way as I grew up and it gave me a moment of clarity in it all. I was shocked.

I couldn't wait to write the other two after getting the first one down on paper. Each letter unveiled buried thoughts and emotions I didn't know I had. It opened my eyes to certain triggers I never knew were even there. Writing to my stepmom I admitted, "I just wish you could have loved me. Even if it was hard to do so, it was all I needed. And you were another reminder to me that I wasn't worthy of that." It made it clear seeing how each relationship crafted space in my journey and had left imprints of shame, guilt, feeling unworthy of love. It was truly incredible, and it was in that moment where I finally opened myself up and saw the potential of what therapy was going to do for me.

After completing this writing exercise, it was the first time I was excited to go into a therapy session. I had spent months dreading every single session until this moment. I had so much I wanted to share and how much I realized just from that small exercise. This would actually be the start of my writing journey, and I owe a lot of my healing and allowing myself to be vulnerable again to it. Once I realized how impactful having this outlet was for me, I started to write almost every night. I would think about a specific moment in my life, or a person or relationship that had a big impact on me. I would tap into the pain, hurt, and trauma that had been buried deep for so many years. And it would just flow as the ink met the paper. At first I did a lot of journaling. I would tell stories about my past or I'd focus on a specific emotion I was feeling and would just put all my thoughts down on paper. I never considered myself as someone who could speak eloquently, or I'd struggle to convey my thoughts out loud with the conviction I felt they carried. I realized if I put the words on a piece of paper, it was a completely different story. Every word carried so much weight that I could feel it lifting off of me little by little. Shedding each and every layer of shame, guilt, resentment, anger, and pain that had found its home within me all these years.

It became apparent that in order for me to truly heal, I had to dig deep and reopen wounds that I had been avoiding my entire life. It was the realization that if I was going to be able to move forward, I was going to have to face the ugliest parts of who I was. And I had to be willing to accept every single one of them. It was who I was, and I would be denying myself a chance of true healing if I continued to avoid and deflect all that was buried beneath the surface. I had started to really trust my therapist and began practicing more authenticity and honesty with her because of all this. I was finally willing to share everything. And I really mean everything. I knew that I could tell her how my thoughts would formulate about a certain situation or experience. Even when I knew what I was thinking was completely unreasonable or invalid, I told her anyway. I had nothing to hide anymore. I knew I would never make the progress I needed to if I continued to wear the masks I had created throughout my life. Trying to protect those parts of me and keep them hidden was only going to delay my progress I was seeing. So, I jumped in completely and never looked back.

I started to see a shift in my everyday life. Things that were hard for me to advocate for were suddenly easy to express. I wasn't filled with fear of rejection, or someone leaving me. I knew I needed to speak up and share my needs and deepest desires. When conflict arose, I didn't go running. I faced it head on, never again feeling I was inadequate to love. It was the jump start to finally finding my voice within. The one of the little girl, so desperate to be loved. I was doing it for her.

Chapter Ten

"When were you last truly happy?" my therapist asked, her question dropping like a stone in still water. I sat frozen, searching through decades of memories and found nothing but an empty void. The silence stretched between us as I realized I couldn't recall a single moment of pure, uncomplicated joy. Not during childhood holidays, not during my wedding day, not even during the births of my children. It was in this moment of painful clarity that I understood I couldn't simply blame others for my unhappiness—I had to finally look inward at my own role in crafting the life I'd been living.

After getting into a groove with my therapy journey, I started to shift my focus to what role I played in all of this. I spent so much of my life blaming those around me for what was happening, that I lacked the self-awareness to see how I was contributing to it all. This was hard to face at times. But I will say it was one of the most imperative steps I ended up taking in order to move forward with my life.

I had been lying about who I was for so long, allowing

others to have power over me so much, that I didn't know who I was anymore. If I wasn't willing to take a step back to see how my own actions and behaviors were impacting my relationships, I was never going to be able to accept my past and work towards a future of true happiness. I was so ashamed of my past and didn't want people to see all of who I was. I lacked vulnerability with most of the people in my life. I didn't feel safe to be myself. Exposing all the cracks in my foundation seemed terrifying. I cared a lot about what other people thought of me, to the point where it would influence what I said and did. I wanted to feel accepted and loved so I said and did what I thought others wanted me to in order for them to accept me. It was exhausting constantly trying to be everything but myself. It wore me down little by little. It was all I had ever known. It took me a long time shifting my focus inward to how I needed to work on myself first and foremost.

My therapist asked me again the question I hadn't yet answered: "When do you feel you were last truly happy?" I just sat there as the words dissolved in my head. In that moment, I couldn't think of anything. Nothing. Memories began to filter through and I would quickly recall only the pain I felt at the time. Reflecting on my childhood was full of hurt as I flipped through holidays, birthdays, school, summer breaks and the memories I was picturing were not happy ones. I remembered the little girl who felt like I never belonged. That I didn't have a mom who loved me enough to stay in my life. That was all I could remember. As I went through the different stages of my life, I couldn't pinpoint any moment of pure happiness within myself. I of course thought of the moments my children were born, how a life-long dream had finally come true. On the inside I wanted to feel happy but all the other pain in my life at the time was looming outside the door of those fragmented happy moments. How could this possibly be? I didn't even know what being happy meant anymore.

Part of the problem was that I didn't think I had any control over my own happiness. I would try to obtain certain things throughout my life thinking it would make me happy. I would think to myself "well if I just made more money, if I had a bigger house, if I buy this new car, when I finally become a mom, when I find someone who loves me, etc." I thought external things would equal a happy life. But I was just chasing thing after thing and the reality was that nothing was ever going to fill the void I had within myself. The deep void of feeling unloved by those I was closest to. It took me a really long time to realize this. I knew I had a long road ahead on defining what happiness meant to me and realizing that I was the only person capable of bringing myself true inner happiness. It's the exact opposite of what I told myself my entire life. It wasn't a shift that was going to happen overnight. It takes work and intention every single day to make the mindset shift that was standing in front of me, staring me right in the face.

I felt I needed certain people in my life to be happy because I was so terrified of being alone. And I was also terrified of failing. At anything honestly. I poured myself into my work because it was the one place in my life I felt like I was getting the validation and reassurance I needed that I wasn't a failure. That I was finally good at something in my life. I was getting really good feedback from my leaders and was always on track to get the next promotion. It was the only thing I had telling me that I was something, so I clung to that, and it became all of who I was.

But once again I was a chameleon taking shape in the midst of it all. I did what I felt others wanted me to do because that was going to get me the attention I was craving. I was practically killing myself working nonstop, trying to say all the right things so I could impress anyone who would listen. I wasn't being true to myself, and I was getting attention by being someone I wasn't. It was all an act like I had been center stage in my entire life. It's just this time, I was seeing a bigger benefit to it all.

The hardest part to admit now is how poorly I treated those around me to get myself further ahead. All of a sudden, my success was blinding me from true authentic relationships and friendships at work. This wasn't who I was deep down. I don't put others to the side to get myself further. It's one of my deepest regrets to this day. I chose my own self-fulfillment over being the kind person I knew I was below the surface. I allowed this sliver of feeling like I was something to someone derail the truest parts of me. I was trying to savor every drop of acknowledgement after feeling like I was chasing after it my entire life.

Outside of feeling successful in my career, I felt like I was a bad friend, a bad wife, a bad mom. I was failing everyone around me, or so it seemed. When in reality, I was the only thing getting in my own way. I was doing so much to control every aspect of my life I forgot how to live it. I couldn't appreciate the happiness of others or their success. I never realized prior to this how much I focused on the failures of others and how that made me feel better about my own life. I still hate admitting that to this day. I wasn't rooting for people anymore—for that promotion at work, a healthy and happy relationship, or reaching a goal that was important to them. And if you are someone who knows the true heart within me, that's just not who I am. But I became consumed with the outcomes of my own life and how they had negatively impacted me—I couldn't focus on anything else.

When we were trying to start a family and were struggling to get pregnant, any friend or family member that announced they were pregnant felt like a punch to the gut. If someone was having great success in their careers, I would pick it apart on why they didn't deserve it. So, when I say at this point in my life I was the worst version of myself—I truly mean it. It was by far the hardest thing to admit and accept in therapy. I was the person I never wanted to be. I was so miserable that I couldn't stand if everyone around me wasn't miserable too. I just wanted to get back to who I knew I really was. To stop being a victim of my past and use all that I had to face throughout life to become a better person. I was letting it have so much power over me that I lost sense of my authentic self.

I started to look at who I was giving my energy to and what I was feeling during and after those interactions. Was it depleting my energy? Was it bringing me more energy? I had to really evaluate where I was putting my time and efforts when it came to family, friendships, work relationships, etc. When I started to surround myself with those who I felt filled my cup, I could feel a shift in my mindset. Their positive mindsets were starting to implant themselves within me. I started to feel excited for others when something great happened in their life. I wanted to be by their side as they celebrated something they had invested a great deal of time into. I was slowly starting to gain the heart I had once again. It was about perspective. And realizing that I had time and love I wanted to give others, but I had to acknowledge where that was going to be received in a way that fulfilled me, not anyone else.

I worked to find what brought me pure joy. Little moments throughout my day that were once filled with scrolling social media and comparing my life to others were now being shifted to pockets of what made me feel good on the inside. I signed up to take some writing classes, hoping to surround myself with others who were on the same mission —to share their words with the world around them. It motivated a creative side of me I didn't know was there, unlocking the potential of self-compassion rather than self-criticism. Instead of watching reality TV at the end of the night, I read books that drove me to finding a purpose or a way of healing. It was interesting to see how quickly my habits and mindset had shifted just from these small changes I was making. I was putting my energy into things that brought me inner happiness, not things that robbed me of it.

I remember when I'd look in the mirror, I'd see this spark in my eyes that hadn't been there for quite some time. Whispering quietly to myself: "You are enough. You've always been enough." Something I tried convincing myself to believe most of my life, but this time it was different. I believed it. Reminding myself that the journey I was on wasn't linear—never a constant move forward. There would be hard days and good days.

This is why I say, if you are someone who is starting therapy, you will need to open yourself up to all the parts of you. Even the ones that are hard to admit about yourself. If you are not self-aware, you will never think you need to change your behaviors or actions that could be contributing to the exact things you are trying to fix. Once you can do this, you will see a turning point in your healing and growth. Just know that you are the only person in control of your own life, your thoughts, and the discipline it can take to keep the voice of negativity out. It won't happen overnight, and it will require a lot of patience and forgiveness for yourself, but I promise you it will be worth it.

Chapter Eleven

I stood at my mother's gravesite, her letter clutched in my hand, those two simple words echoing in my mind: "I'm sorry." Words I had waited a lifetime to hear, delivered too late for her to see my tears or feel my embrace. As I placed wildflowers on the fresh earth, I felt something shift inside me—the tight knot of anger I had carried for decades began to loosen. God had blessed me with a forgiving heart, but until that moment, I hadn't understood its true power—not just to free others from blame, but to release myself from the prison of resentment I had built.

God blessed me with a forgiving heart—something I've come to completely admire about myself. Despite the moments in my life when I've felt resentment at times, I've always been able to look the person in the eye and offer them forgiveness. It hasn't always been easy to do, especially at the time in my life when I felt at my lowest. But with the work I've put into myself, forgiveness has been at the center of it all. I had to reflect a ton on some of the key relationships I've had throughout my life, a lot of the ones I've mentioned so far.

When I was in those times of my life, I was perceiving everything from the lens of what I felt and understood was happening in that exact moment. I didn't have the ability to look beyond the actions other than seeing them as an intentional plan to hurt me. Now I've realized how much our footprint throughout our lives shape us into who we are and why we react certain ways to emotions, circumstances, and people. Sometimes it's not about focusing on the direct action or behavior that has hurt you. Instead, it's more about understanding the reasons behind the action.

Most of the time, the people in our lives are not intentionally trying to hurt us. Sure, there are exceptions to that, but those that truly love and care for us don't go out of their way to hurt us. However, in any relationship or friendship, you have to understand that there is always the chance that you will hurt one another at some point and to some degree. It's what makes our relationships human. It's those moments that can test our faith and ability to forgive. To know that they've done something that has caused us pain and yet, still be able to move forward and not continue to carry that pain into every aspect of the relationship. Once I was able to grasp that concept, it unlocked so much for me and the forgiveness I have been able to give to others and, more importantly, to myself.

I shared a lot about certain people throughout my life and how much I struggled at those times to understand their perspective. Regarding my dad, I felt it was all his fault for my mom leaving us and that he didn't care enough to give us the emotional support that we needed. I had to look at it in a completely different way. Throughout therapy and focusing specifically on inner child work, I learned that there is a cycle we all go through as we go throughout life. We learn how to manage our emotions, how we communicate those feelings to other people, and how we react. These are all learned habits that our parents learned from their parents, that they learned from their parents, etc. I had to peel back the layers my dad was under as he went through one of the most painful times of his life. Just like I was trying to learn how to just purely survive, so was he. It opened up a whole new way of thinking and reflecting on that time in his life. Understanding that we all hold on to pain in our own ways, and how we grew up learning to navigate that is what teaches us as adults. My dad was only going off of what he knew from his own upbringing. Being able to put myself in his shoes gave me the perspective I needed all those years ago. And through that, I was able to forgive him after so many years of holding onto the thought that he was doing this all intentionally.

I remember watching an interview with a therapist on social media and they were saying, "One of the biggest ways to be happier in life is to stop blaming our parents and forgive them." At first, it made me think, well how could that make you happier? I realized what he meant was that as we grow into adults, we hold onto things that our parents said or did at the time, and we have a hard time letting go of it. What we don't realize is there is so much that goes into how we are raised and why. What was the dynamic of our parents' upbringing? We do better when we know better but sometimes, we are faced with what we grew up with because that is all we know. Our parents didn't have any bit of information available at their fingerprints like parents do today. The world is a completely different place now and at that time, our parents were doing what they thought was right and only with what they knew. We don't always see the struggles they are faced with and how much that can impact how they raise us as kids.

I had a conversation with my dad one day, sitting at their lake house drinking our morning cup of coffee together. Something that we've bonded on over the years. I could see a sense of peace in his eyes as he overlooked the lake lot that he spent so many years building as their safe place. It was a moment of clarity for me. He finally found the peace he was looking for in his life. He shared a thought about me and my brother. How he was so proud of how far we had come despite all that was stacked up against us. He said to me, "I'm just so glad that you both turned out okay. The thought of you two not, used to keep me up at night for many years." That moment was one I'll hold on to forever. The moment that my heart was changed by him once again. Seeing all he did and the weight of worry he carried, now drifting away just like the lake tides we sat and listened to quietly that morning.

I had to have a moment of that within my own journey of motherhood. I wasn't showing up the way I knew I could and the way my own kids deserved. I had to do better. They deserved it. And I got the help I needed to be able to do that. But I now know that my dad was doing the best with what he could at the time, and I can't continue to have this internal struggle with accepting that. And honestly, the second I got to the point of being able to do that, I instantly felt a huge weight lifted off me.

The same goes for my mom. When she passed away and I read the letter she left for my brother and I, I saw a different side of her story than what I was allowing myself to see. She had so many internal struggles at the time of my parents' divorce. She had really low self-esteem, she didn't feel loved by others in her life, and she was severely depressed. She had no idea how to cope with all that in a healthy way. So, she looked for validation in the wrong places, she used substances to numb the pain she was in so she didn't have to think about it. And once she became an addict, it completely took over the way she thought and what she did. She was sick. But at that time, I took everything she did as a direct intentional action to hurt everyone around her. She wasn't herself anymore, but I refused to see it the way it really was.

And reading her letter, I could feel it in her words, how regretful she was and how much it weighed on her throughout her life. Her mentioning how much she realized she missed out on in our lives, how she never got to meet her own grandchildren, she never got to see us get married and have our babies. She missed some of the most important moments of our lives and she was finally realizing it was due to her own actions. She never took accountability for what she had done until that letter. As I read every single word, I felt like I was shedding a layer of myself with each one. The weight of her actions holding me down my entire life suddenly didn't seem so heavy. Forgiving her felt like releasing an anchor I had been carrying for years.

Her entire letter had regret written all over it. She wasn't able to forgive herself for what she did either, and the least I can do now is offer her the forgiveness I truly believe she deserves. Yes, she made some poor decisions throughout her life that affected me greatly, but I know now that her disease with her addiction wasn't allowing her to think and act the way the true version of herself typically would. It wasn't my mom anymore and I know that. I don't think she would've ever in her right mind done what she did if she wasn't struggling so much. I've accepted that and have freed myself of the prison I kept myself in that was preventing me from breaking free of the pain she held me hostage to.

And then you have my sister. Although her and I encountered a lot of the same struggles growing up, they impacted us both differently. Adding in the loss of her child and feeling as though she wasn't accepted into our blended family. She had a lot that she was carrying with her every day. At the time of her death, I felt like she deliberately knew how much it would hurt me but decided to go through with it anyway. I took what she did so personally, and it wasn't until I realized that more than likely in that moment she wasn't thinking about anyone but herself. She was focused only on the pain she was feeling, not the pain that her actions were going to cause to those around her. How she got to the point that ending her life seemed like her only way out. She was fighting more within herself than I think anyone will ever know. She wasn't leaving to hurt everyone around her. She made that decision to end the pain she believed she would never be able to escape.

I blamed myself for years after she died that I didn't do enough to help her. This was something I talked about a lot during therapy and what it helped me realize was that no matter how hard I tried to help her, she had to want the help too. You can't force an alcoholic to get better. They have to want that for themselves, and my sister was just never there. She wasn't ready to get the help she needed and there was nothing I could do. It was honestly freeing once I realized all this.

I had to learn to forgive her for making a decision in that

moment that unfortunately was permanent. You don't realize the aftermath you will leave those you love in when you do what she did. It was a long road to get there but I know that she had so much love for me, would've done anything to protect me at all costs. If she could, she would take on any pain herself if it would spare me any ounce of it. I've been able to obtain so much more peace about my relationship and memory of my sister now. I can look back and be thankful for all the time I did have with her and not focus so much on the time that I've lost. I know people often say that suicide is one of the most selfish things you can do, and to a degree that's true. All they are thinking about in those moments are themselves, but I think that's also the one way we can understand it more. They aren't thinking about their family, friends, or significant others. If they did, I'm guessing a lot more people wouldn't go through with it.

And this is where forgiveness can be difficult—when we can't ask the questions flooding our minds as a way to understand "why" so that we can somehow grasp the reality more. You have to forgive them blindly, knowing you will more than likely never have the answers. But that is the true example of forgiveness. When we don't have all the things telling us to do it. But we do it because we know it will give us the peace we need to move on.

Lastly, I want to share the forgiveness I had to give to myself. This was the most important out of all of them. Looking back on my life I know that there were relationships, people, and situations I didn't handle the way I would've liked. When I was struggling as a first time mom, I carried so much guilt around with how my kids viewed me as they grew up. Did they think I wasn't giving them enough? Was I always letting them down? I beat myself up a lot for all of it. And fast forward to the time in my life when I was the most broken I had ever been. I know I could've been a better friend, wife, mom, daughter, all of the above. But I couldn't continue punishing myself for things I couldn't change anymore. Breaking the cycles I grew up with became more important than ever. Offering forgiveness to my own children when they made mistakes. Helping them see they were safe to make mistakes and that my love wouldn't waver depending on the conditions.

I couldn't go back and change the outcomes, but I had to focus on understanding how my own life experiences shaped me into the person I was in each and every one of those moments in my life. I needed to understand my "why" and how I can be more aware of it going forward so I can choose a different path. I started practicing reflection every night to see where I hadn't shown up the way I wanted to. And as I would identify these moments, whether it was a situation I lost my patience with my kids, I didn't reach out to a friend to check on them as they were going through a hard time, I didn't give my full attention in a conversation with a co-worker. I would replay the events throughout my day and recognize when I was falling short. And instead of just acknowledging the moments, I would practice forgiving myself for each and every one. Understanding why I didn't show up the way I wanted to, and allowing myself the space to learn from it, grow and move forward without holding myself as a hostage to every mistake I was making. Something I had done throughout most of my life. I'd make a mistake and I would think about it obsessively and beat myself up for it. I couldn't let it go and it was brewing so much guilt within me. It was a large contributor to when I didn't love myself anymore.

As I've continued to grow in my faith, I've seen how much forgiveness can offer a person or situation and it's been the most at peace I've been in my entire life. It actually feels good to be able to forgive someone when they've done you wrong. And I've seen what it's done for those individuals as well. There's something beautiful when you can look at someone and give them the gift of forgiveness. It's them seeing there are still good people in the world, that we make mistakes and people will forgive you for them. More importantly, that God forgives you. That's been one of the most rewarding parts of all of this. All I could hope is that those I've forgiven can see this gift and one day offer it to someone else—or even to themselves.

Chapter Twelve

Have you ever heard the phrase, "You are either growing together or growing apart?" I've heard this a few times in reference to relationships—and it's true. When you think about all the time you spend with your spouse or partner throughout your lifetime, it's impossible to be the exact same person you were the day you met. Of course, there are certain characteristics about a person that carry throughout our lives, but overall you change and evolve as your life goes on. It's not a bad thing—it can actually be a really good thing. The point is that when you are in a marriage or relationship with someone else, both of you are going to change over time—that's called growth. The real question is: are you growing together, or are the changes pulling you apart? And have you noticed?

One of the biggest learning moments for me as I progressed in therapy and learning more about myself was that I was making a conscious effort to grow and change for the better. That didn't seem to be the journey my husband was on. As I started to gain more self-awareness, I built a level of confidence in myself that I never had previously. I started to understand what I really wanted out of life and my relationships. I began to figure out what type of partner I truly needed and desired. It became apparent that my marriage was not fulfilling me emotionally and it was consistently triggering wounds that I was trying to heal.

As I started to realize all the trauma I had faced throughout my life, I realized that there were certain aspects of a relationship that I now knew I needed. They weren't something I understood when I was a young college kid entering into my relationship with my husband. What I needed was someone who wasn't going to use my weaknesses against me for their own gains. Do I think my husband loved me? Of course, I just don't think he knew how to love me. And in return, I wasn't loving him the way he deserved either.

There was a specific moment in our marriage where it became obvious to me how unhappy we both were. Around our 10th wedding anniversary, we went on a trip together to celebrate. It was our first trip together without kids in years and we planned to meet another couple from our college days there as well. You would think in the days leading up to a 10th wedding anniversary trip, one would be excited to spend some time with their spouse. For some reason, I just had this pit in my stomach, almost like a feeling of dread. I ignored it and convinced myself it was nothing.

We got to Las Vegas and although I was looking forward to seeing some amazing shows, eating good food, and having some time to decompress from our busy life, I found myself just wanting to spend time with our friends more than I did with my own husband. I felt like we were so disconnected from one another and were having a hard time enjoying the time together just as a couple. I mean, in a typical day of our life we were usually figuring out what was for dinner, who was going to take the kids to their next doctor's appointment, shuffling kids to and from their activities. Outside of that we didn't put any effort into just us. We were going through the motions of life and were leaving each other at the bottom of our priority list. And that was a glaring realization on this trip.

One of the nights we were there, my husband and our friend decided they wanted to spend the rest of the evening after dinner at the casino. So, my friend begged me to go out dancing with her and as reluctant as I was, I told her I would go. It ended up being one of the best nights of the trip. Her and I had so much fun together and were meeting a lot of new people throughout the course of the night. In hindsight, I feel like I enjoyed this night in particular because I wasn't spending the evening with my husband. And that is so sad to even write. I never want to feel like that about my partner. It was just so glaringly obvious at this point though. I never felt strongly connected to him in our entire relationship, it brought me back to my childhood where I felt I couldn't express my emotions and needs. It was an extension of the pain I had been feeling almost my entire life. There was always something holding us back from getting there and I never knew what it was.

While we were out dancing, we met this great group of people and ended up spending a lot of our night with them. They were teaching us how to salsa dance and there was one of them in particular I started to feel a connection growing with. We danced and shared drinks as he asked me a lot about my life, my marriage, and shared a lot of his own journey through marriage and divorce with me as well. As the night continued, the bright lights of the dance floor, the smell of sweet sweat and alcohol lingering, I felt like it was only him and I in the room. It was a moment where I felt desired by someone, understood in a way I never had before in my life. Each word I shared with him you could see it carefully making a home within him. Taking each morsel of information and building an understanding of who I was. I felt like the only priority to him, and it was something I had been craving in my own relationship. I didn't want the night to end. I found myself wanting to spend more time with this person, but I knew the night was about to be over. It was a moment where I had to snap myself back into the reality I was in. Not wanting the feeling of this to go away, I knew I had to remove myself from the situation before anything else could happen. I may not have been happy in my marriage, but cheating was something I could never do. I did love my husband and cared deeply for him, it wasn't a situation I wanted to continue putting myself in, so my friend and I decided it was time to leave.

When we left the dance club for the evening the same group of people we spent most of the evening with ended up seeing us in our hotel lobby after we left. They came to talk to us some more and the one who had been showing interest in me throughout the night ended up pulling me aside and asking me for my number. I told him I didn't think that was a good idea. He then asked me a strange question, he said, "Are you happily married?" I laughed it off and said, "Of course I am" and he said, "Okay, okay I will leave you alone then." We said goodnight to them all and went our separate ways.

As I was walking back to my room that night, his question kept coming back to me. I had a moment where I asked

myself, "Am I actually happy in my marriage?" It was difficult when I realized I couldn't remember the last time I felt
happy in my marriage. Most of the time, I felt like my
husband was borderline just tolerating me and it seemed
obvious he felt I was a difficult person to love. I always felt
like I was an inconvenience to him. We were just going
through the motions, and we stopped making each other a
priority, and that's a stretch to even say we ever did that to
begin with. I think from the start we were having issues and
just never addressed them, or we would wait for them to
blow up to a point where we would have a terrible fight, he
would threaten a divorce, I would give in and take the blame
so he wouldn't leave me, and then we would rinse and repeat
from there. Everything we did was purely transactional and
not because we actually wanted to show love to one another.
We never took the time to understand how each one of us
not only wanted to be loved, but how we needed to be loved.

I left Las Vegas feeling so discouraged. I knew I had to
say something to him about it, but I wanted to wrap my head
around what was all going through my mind at the time. I
took a few days to reflect on how I had been feeling during
our trip and I finally had to admit to myself that our relationship hadn't been great for a really long time. Sure, all
marriages go through hard times, especially when you are in
the thick of raising a young family, jobs are stressful, your
schedule is packed with activity after activity. This wasn't
the scenario though. I finally was realizing how unloved I
felt. I didn't feel appreciated for all I did to keep our family
running and our household operating. I took on the full
mental load of everything and never felt like I was appreciated for what I did. I felt like I was difficult to love for a lot of
reasons, that I was so broken, and it was impossible to love

someone like me. I saw the resentment that I had been storing away for a really long time. This wasn't all I realized though. I started to see that I was always wanting to change my husband. I didn't love him unconditionally and I knew how unfair that was to him. He shouldn't have to change who he is in order for me to love him. No one deserves that.

I started to see the entire picture and that I don't think I ever loved him the way he deserved, or I should have from the beginning. I accepted less than I needed in order to have a sense of security. To think that or even say it out loud left me completely shook. How could I have done this? How unfair of me to feel this way and never see it or admit it for all these years. Through no fault of my own, I don't think I was ever going to see it until I started working through the trauma from my past. The broken version of me was willing to accept less than I knew I deserved because at that time in my life I didn't think I deserved more. I do want to say that my life wasn't terrible. Trust me, I saw first-hand with my mom how much worse it could be. But I would be lying to myself and doing me and my kids a disservice to continue accepting a reality that wasn't what was best for me.

And that's when I knew my marriage was over a long time ago. I just finally got to a place where I was able to see the dynamic of what it was.

Once I got to that point, I knew I had to talk to him about it. I was sitting in our living room on the opposite side of the couch from him like we usually did. The kids were all soundly asleep in their beds and the darkness from the night filled the hollow echoes of our living room. It felt cold as I looked around the room. I sat and picked at the skin on my lips for over an hour trying to muster up the courage to say something. I finally looked at him and said, "I think we need to talk." I could already feel the water filling up my eyes as I looked at him and asked, "Are you happy?" He gave me a confused look back and said, "Yeah why are you asking me that? Are you not?" His face went from normal to white in that one statement. A look of almost terror flashing in his eyes. I could feel the rush of heat flow through my entire body as I looked at him and said, "No." When that one word left my lips, I could see the despair on his face as the reality of what I just said started to sink in. Both of us sitting and just staring at one another. Not knowing what to say next. I felt complete emptiness inside. How could one word feel like your entire world had been stripped from within you? You never imagine yourself getting to this place and then all of the sudden you are there. In disbelief that this is actually happening. I felt relieved and terrified all at the same time.

As we let the words we shared linger in the stale, dark moment, he seemed so blindsided, and I was honestly so confused by that. Everything he did and his actions told me otherwise. He seemed so miserable sharing a life with me. Like anything I did or said seemed to annoy him constantly. I told him I felt like we hadn't been happy for a really long time, and I didn't know what to do. I asked him to take some time to really think about it and that we could discuss every-thing more once we both had some time to think and really reflect. I didn't know this at the time but that moment, that conversation would end up being the beginning of the end. It was the first night we would sleep in separate bedrooms in our entire marriage. I had no idea the path we were about to take and there was nothing that would've prepared me for what was next.

Part Four

Finding Purpose

I stood in the quiet of my own undoing
Surrounded by the weight of absence
As if the world had forgotten to hold me
What I once thought defined me
Now seemed so distant
For a while I believed the emptiness was all
    there was
That I was hollow
But in that space of nothing
Something began to stir
Not a voice, but a presence
Deep within, unbroken
It wasn't loud or demanding
Just a steady pull
A reminder of what I had buried
Beneath the surface of life
I began to listen, swallowed by the silence

The parts I had neglected
The strength I had forgotten
I had thought I was lost
In the stillness I rediscovered myself
Not just the version I had once known
Something deeper
And in that quiet truth
I found the depth I had long sought outside
Waiting within me
Untouched by time

Chapter Thirteen

After finally saying out loud that I wasn't happy, I was filled with an immense amount of sadness and relief at the same time. It's like the moment you've been under-water holding your breath, and you finally reach the surface and take that first gasping breath. I felt like I had been held underwater for years and could finally breathe again. This didn't make it easy though. We had countless conversations about what we should do next. We agreed at the time to try and fix our issues and move forward together.

We started couples therapy to navigate our next steps. But after spending time in our own individual therapy and then our time in therapy together, I realized that for me to move forward with him, I had to focus on fixing some of the deep-rooted issues within myself. I had pushed them down for so long, and it affected the way I was showing up for our marriage. I knew that those needed to be addressed so I could feel like I could move forward as a unit.

This was really hard for my husband to understand. He

questioned why I couldn't work on both at the same time. To be honest, I was overwhelmed. I was trying to take some time to look at myself within, understand some of the habits I had formed over the course of my life, and what triggered the behaviors I was desperately trying to stop. And at the same time, I was being asked to completely overhaul our entire relationship, work a full-time demanding job, and care for three young kids who also needed their mom. I felt like there weren't enough hours in the day to do everything being asked of me. There was so much pressure that I felt like nothing was being accomplished because I was spreading myself too thin. I had to be firm with needing time to focus on myself.

I started to look for retreats that I could attend to help give me some time to disconnect from the chaos of life but also allow a moment to reconnect with myself. I ended up finding a retreat in Puerto Rico that was titled, "Reparent Your Inner Child." The description covered exactly every-thing that I was looking for. I didn't hesitate and booked it right away. I had every intention of going alone but there was a pull for me to ask one of my closest friends to go with me. I knew she had been struggling with some of her own things from growing up and her current family dynamic, so I asked if she wanted to go with me. She jumped at the chance, and just like that, I wasn't going alone. I was so excited about it, yet apprehensive at the same time. It was intimidating to think about spending multiple days in a secluded part of another country with complete strangers, pouring out every bit of trauma I had encountered in my life. Yet, it was exactly what I needed.

The concept of the retreat was something that was a bit

new to me. I had talked about inner child work a little with my therapist, but I didn't quite understand how much you can learn about yourself within the process. My therapist prepped me for the retreat and agreed that it was the perfect thing for me to do. When I boarded the plane to head there, I had no idea how much my life was about to change.

When we got to Puerto Rico, we had made plans to drive out to the retreat location with a couple locals from the island. We had spent the first couple days in San Juan taking in all the food, music, history, and architecture. We then met up with a couple that was heading to the retreat and immediately grew a bond with them the minute we jumped in their car. They drove us the couple hours out to the beautiful mountains and as we approached the resort we would be staying at, I instantly felt at peace.

I couldn't believe how beautiful this place was. And the people there made us feel like we were right at home. As we were walking to our personal hut we would be sleeping in, I looked out across the mountains, and my eyes filled with tears. This was exactly what my heart and soul had needed.

During the first gathering we did as an entire group, our retreat leader shared what the next few days were going to look like and how we were going to be spending our time. Then she had us go around the entire circle and share what it was we were hoping to get out of the retreat. It was scary opening up that quickly to a large group of complete strangers, but it was comforting to hear how many others were hoping to find some healing and growth during our time there. Each person craved some type of healing from their past. Every single one of us different but the same.

Before the retreat, I told myself that after each day of the retreat, I would take time to write and reflect on what I learned and took away from the sessions. I wanted to document all my emotions and thoughts because I knew it was going to be a lot to take in. I wanted to have those reminders when I left about what the time really meant for me. I had been doing a lot of journaling leading up to this, but this retreat would be what ended up spearheading my full-on love for writing poetry.

The three days of the retreat were intense to say the least. The sessions were set up to slowly peel back layer after layer of your childhood and how it impacts the adult in you today. I learned so much about the lack of emotional safety I felt as a child and how I could still learn how to reparent that version of myself. I became so much more aware of my triggers, how I typically responded to these and how I needed to show up for myself as the parent I always needed back then. To help heal those wounds I've left open for so long. But what I also realized was just how much work I still had to do. It was humbling in a way, putting the cracks that I thought were repaired on full display.

The retreat helped me uncover even more of my past that I had been masking and now it was my time to rip those masks completely off to face the pain I hid for all my life. I could see the long healing journey I still had in front of me, but it confirmed that I was on the right path. I could see how much growth I had already accomplished within myself. As I would listen to others share their stories, it was one of the first times I felt seen. Here I was surrounded by others who were struggling because of their past. Every person's story was their own but there was a sense of belonging that came with it. I felt like a real person in their eyes, no longer just a shell of who I was. A whole person with a story to tell, a story only I knew.

The last night I was there, I pulled out my notebook to start writing about the day. I ended up writing a letter to myself that I didn't know I would end up sharing in our closing circle the next day. Similar to the first day, our retreat leader had us all go around and share what we took away from our time there. It was an emotional moment for many of us. I hadn't spoken up a lot. Instead, I was taking in the stories from others and listening to how their childhood was affecting them similar to me. But I was scared to be so vulnerable with so many people who knew nothing about me.

I panicked for a bit as each person went on to share the magnitude of their learnings, I kept thinking to myself, *how are you possibly going to be able to convey the healing you just experienced? And how can you say it so eloquently like everyone else seems to be able to do?* And then I looked over and saw my notebook sitting next to me and remembered what I wrote to myself the night before. I decided I would just read that. My hands were sweating as I turned the page that I poured my thoughts onto just hours before. I took a deep breath and here is what I shared:

Puerto Rico, you will have a piece of my heart forever. I booked this trip back in December when I was in a really tough place and feeling a little lost. I needed a chance to find "me" again, reconnect with myself and do a little soul search-ing. I saw a retreat that was here, and it couldn't have been a better fit for me and the journey I was on. I took it as a sign, booked it, and never looked back. They say there are trips you take that can completely change your life. This was one of those for me. I laughed. I cried. I opened myself up to old wounds. I healed. I grew. I learned. I got uncomfortable. It took me an incredibly long time to realize that pain and trauma grow deep within you and pushing them down will only cause more issues in how you show up for yourself and others. So, this was a chance for me to disconnect and truly focus on myself and the healing I really needed to do. I've regained a tremendous amount of self-love through this process and shed a few of my old layers to leave behind. Lastly, I want to share a quote that I wrote down the first day of the retreat that really stuck with me: "Once you fully know and understand yourself, you can change everything." It's never too late to change your life. And that's exactly what I'm going to do.

When I finished reading this out loud to the group, I heard someone say "wow." There were tears in people's eyes. It was in that exact moment I realized how much I wanted to share more of my writing. I felt like I could write so beautifully and make sense of all the chaos going on in my head.

When I returned home, I walked in the door and my husband was waiting for me. I was grateful that he encouraged me to take the trip and spend some time on myself and my healing. He never once made me feel guilty for booking the trip and taking time away from our busy lives. But I think he was hoping I'd go there and come back with clarity on our marriage. If anything, I was more confused than ever. Something that stood out to me was that I had this pit in my stomach coming back home. I had been missing my kids and couldn't wait to squeeze them all. But when my husband came to welcome me home and hug me, I felt nothing. I knew more than ever in that moment that I didn't love him the way I knew I should or the way he deserved. I think he could see it in my eyes, and his hopefulness went straight to agony in that moment.

We would end up trying to hold on a few more months, but in that time, we just continued to grow further and further apart. It was wearing on the both of us at this point and I knew that the resentment I had built over the years had already poisoned everything we had. I just couldn't see us getting to a place in our relationship where we were both feeling fulfilled and giving each other the partner I know we both deserved. This was the moment I knew I had to take a step back and think about not just how I was feeling, but what I was capable of giving to him going forward.

When we'd spend time apart, I couldn't ignore the peace I felt in those moments. Like I could breathe, a sliver of happiness showing up within me once again. I reflected a lot in those last few months, but it only became clearer how incompatible we were for one another. I couldn't continue to ask him to be someone he wasn't. And I couldn't continue to pretend to love someone that I didn't in the way I should. It just wasn't fair anymore. Not just to me but to him and our kids. They deserved a better example of what loving your spouse truly means. What we were giving them was an example of two people who barely tolerated one another.

As we grew further and further apart, any ounce of care for one another started to diminish. Each conversation over-flowed with more hurt and anger as we started to see the writing on the wall. The last hope we were both holding onto fell through our fingertips. We started the painful process of filing for our divorce. There were a lot of big decisions we had to make, but one thing I will say, despite all the pain and hurt we were both feeling, we were able to keep our kids at the center of every decision we made.

Parenting was always something we actually did do well together. He is a great dad and he knows I am a good mom. We both know how much our kids deserve to have both of us in their lives equally. We worked through custody, finances, housing, etc. and were able to keep every single bit of it amicable. Neither one of us was trying to ruin the life of the other. At the end of the day, the other person was going to be caring for our kids fifty percent of the time and trying to ruin them financially and emotionally wasn't going to set our kids up for the best environment they deserved.

I am so proud of us for being able to put our own differences aside and continue working together as a parenting team to do what was best for our kids in a circumstance that was difficult no matter what we did. Many people commended us for how well we handled the filing process and how we were going to separate the life we had spent over ten years of marriage building. It wasn't easy and those were some of the darkest, loneliest months of my life. But we did it. And we continue to show up for our kids and each other in any way we can to this day.

It's something I hope our kids can see and appreciate one day. Even though we put them through a divorce, I know they know how much both of us love them and will always work together to give them everything we are able to. Sadness comes with a marriage ending, even if it's the best thing for everyone involved. Seeing how we could show up for each other the way we did, even when we were both hurting, gave me a sense of peace with the decision. I knew that things would never be the same again, but I became hopeful that we both were going to walk into a time in our lives of rebuilding our own foundations, loving ourselves, and becoming the best version of ourselves. With all that at the forefront, I knew the best was yet to come for us both.

However, those months, to this day, were some of the hardest I have ever faced. I'm grateful for the community of friends and family that rallied around me when I felt completely broken. The countless hours I'd cry to one of them over the phone, trying so hard to be strong while feeling like I was falling apart. I don't know how I would've made it through that time without them. Their support, love, encouragement, and presence kept me going. Yet even with so much support surrounding me, it was one of the loneliest times of my life. I felt misunderstood, judged, questioned. I had crafted the image of a perfect life, and no one could understand how we had arrived at this point.

It's interesting—in moments of tremendous suffering, you might be surprised who shows up for you and who doesn't. During this time, I lost friends I thought I'd have for a lifetime, while gaining new ones who didn't hesitate to be there when I least expected it. This eye-opening experience grounded me in the friendships God knew I needed. Once again, He was showing me His plans for me. To the friends who stood with me: thank you. You protected a heart that wasn't yours to protect. You picked me up when I was at my lowest and showered me with unwavering support. For that, I will be forever grateful.

Those final months living under the same roof together were not easy. Trying to figure out life beyond the marriage but all while still living together was hard. My focus was, find a place that will feel like home to your kids. I was so sad to be leaving our current home, but I knew it was the smartest option for me to leave and find something smaller that I would be able to manage on my own. I was looking forward to the fresh start but was also completely terrified. I hadn't been alone for so long and had no idea what it was going to be like. All I knew is that I wanted to start this new chapter of my learning to spend some time alone, rediscovering myself a bit. I didn't plan on trying to date anyone right away and just focus on getting myself and the kids settled into our new normal. But God had other plans for me.

Chapter Fourteen

As I approached this new chapter in my life, I kept asking myself, "How are you ever going to find someone to fall in love with again?" I was terrified to be starting over and had no idea what the future would hold. I was figuring out who I was again and didn't feel confident to jump back into dating right away. Those thoughts filled with doubt would flood my mind constantly. "Are you going to meet someone who truly knows how to love you?" "Will you be enough?" "How are my kids going to feel seeing me with someone else?" It was a constant battle that I would fight.

I felt so broken at that time in my life that opening my heart to someone else seemed impossible. I remember hearing something about the first relationship after your divorce will often break you more than the divorce itself. Sitting in the aftermath of divorce, I couldn't imagine that being true. It was one of the most painful experiences I had ever been through, and I didn't know if I would ever endure another heartbreak like I just had. I wanted to protect myself from all of that. I told myself to take as long as possible before I would even think about dating. But sometimes God has other plans for us. Just as I was about to move into my new house, I met someone who would completely change my life.

It was a situation I never thought I would encounter. I was traveling for work and ended up meeting someone while I was on this trip. The moment felt serendipitous. A story of two people who meet one another in a place neither of them even live. Knowing what the universe needed to align for that exact moment to take place seemed surreal. It felt too good to be true. When I wasn't even looking, along came the person I had been searching my entire life for.

That night we exchanged stories of the trials we faced in our marriages; what it looked like on the other side of divorce and the connection we shared made me feel like I had known this person my entire life. There were times I would tell him that there was a place in my heart I felt was there my entire life just waiting for him to fill it. It was a moment where I felt safe with someone for the first time in a long time. We spent the entire night talking, and when he left I didn't think I was ever going to hear from him again. So, when I got a text message from him later that night, I was shocked.

Those first few weeks of our relationship still feel surreal when I think about it. He lived in Tennessee while I lived in Minnesota, and yet, I wasn't hesitant at all about how difficult that would be for us to navigate. We both had kids, and we both knew it wasn't going to be easy building a relationship with one another. But I couldn't ignore the fact that I felt like we were both offering each other every-thing we were looking for in a partner. We were mirrors in each other's stories; when I looked at him, I could see myself. Both broken from our past, but hopeful for our future.

Something that stood out to me from the very beginning was that I was able to be completely open with this person. There was never a moment where he made me feel bad for the feelings that I had. A feeling that was so foreign to me. My marriage had made me believe that my feelings were too much, that I was too much. This was different though. I felt a gentleness from him that I had craved for as long as I could remember. All the walls I had slowly built came crashing down around me. Leaving me feeling the most vulnerable I have ever been in my entire life. It was one of the most terrifying yet empowering experiences. I felt alive again. A permanent smile placed where my tears used to drown me. I felt like I finally found the love I had been searching for.

Despite the distance between us, the future looked promising for us. I would lay in bed at night and wonder how I was able to find this person so quickly after my divorce. That this person opened everything I had closed off from the world my whole life almost in an instant. It was an intense connection, often feeling chaotic at times. Everything was passionate, emotional, and filled with a level of intensity that I couldn't understand how this was missing in my relationships prior. When I was with him, I felt like I could do anything. He supported me in every way someone possibly could—emotionally, physically, and mentally. He gave me a foundation of hope that seemed so unattainable at that time in my life. Every doubt that once lived inside me evolved into a sliver of hope that filled my entire soul.

The contrast between this relationship and my marriage was glaring. Here I had someone I could be open with, fully transparent and vulnerable. My emotions felt seen, and it was like I could be my true and complete self. My marriage held me captive in a cage of my own worth. Barely able to break free from the burdens I felt placed around me. Hiding behind a perception I created. It felt like I went from one extreme to the other. I thought this was a sign that this relationship was meant for me to walk into. That it was going to be completely different, and in a lot of ways it was.

But I had no idea the new pain I would be exposed to in this new relationship. Feeling safety and fear all at the same time was leaving me in a constant state of confusion, doubt, and worry—something that, over time, began to wear me down to my bones again. All the armor I had carefully covered myself in was shattered and left me with nothing left. Just me fully exposed and vulnerable, placing all my trust into someone I felt would protect my heart in ways I hadn't experienced before.

But the peak came crashing down just as quickly as it started. This was when the lies I was being told were unveiled—and it was just the tip of the iceberg. Lies that cut so deep I didn't even recognize this type of pain. Every hope I had, our future I envisioned, all became a tiny morsel of reality. As someone who forgives quickly, I held on to any of the positive that I could. I was willing to do just about anything to make this relationship work. I told myself this person was so much better than the lies he was telling me. That he truly loved me and was never intending to hurt me. I convinced myself that this wasn't truly who he was deep down. I felt so strongly that the person I met and fell in love with was the truest version of the heart he held. And that the hurt and pain he suffered from led him down a path where lying was the only way he saw out. Him not feeling seen, heard, and understood from those he was the closest to, caused him to push people away who wanted to love him.

Over the course of the next year, it would bring me on a rollercoaster that I couldn't escape. The hope I had for this person to change was the only thing keeping me hanging on. I convinced myself things would change. That I was different, and he loved me enough to never hurt me again. He would end our relationship over and over again and then we would quickly find our way back together again. Feeling like the universe would do anything to not keep us apart. I was blinded by the potential I saw in this person. But the reality is that you can't want something for someone more than they want it for themselves. I had prayed for him to want to change. To heal the wounds that were so deep within him so he could see the love he truly deserved. I wanted to be that person for him. But all it did was destroy the best parts of me in the process.

There was a final moment of clarity after a year and a half of emotional chaos. One that was hard to face at the time. I had never encountered the level of betrayal I faced with him, and I had no idea how I was going to come back from that. I knew I could forgive him, but could I trust him again? I had to take a step back and look at the relationship as a whole. I knew I loved this person, without an ounce of doubt in my mind. I loved the parts of him that he hated, every last thing about him I adored. The battles he faced within himself were too profound for him to continue to ignore. Because of this, I felt like he didn't love himself enough to love anyone else fully and completely. It caused him to push those that loved him the most away, feeling as though he didn't deserve it. I could empathize with this, knowing exactly what that feels like. I was there for some of his darkest days, crawling to the bottomless pit he found himself in. Loving him every step of the way. But in turn, his lies continued to grow and every fear I had came true. I felt betrayed, humiliated, hurt, and unworthy. All the things I had been running from my whole life finally caught back up to me. This relationship ripped every old wound wide open again, all while creating new ones at the same time.

The level of pain I felt was new to me. I thought I had experienced heartbreak before, but this was different. The heart I opened to this person became the collateral damage to their own pain and selfishness. Recognizing all of this was one of the hardest parts.

During all of this I had a realization, that for most of my life I was in a state of chaos. This was so familiar to me that if my relationships or life wasn't chaotic, I didn't know what to do with myself. I became so comfortable with this that when there was a moment of peace, I couldn't sit in it. Peace was so foreign to me that it felt wrong. I thrived in chaos, and it was exactly the setting of this relationship.

Although our love and connection to one another was unmatched, the chaos of our circumstances, the lies and betrayal, felt normal to me at times. I ignored it because I didn't know how to exist without it. By the time I had endured so much hurt, I finally could see the toll this was taking on my emotional, physical, and mental wellbeing. I was utterly exhausted, and my body was starting to shut down. I could sleep for days and never felt recovered. I was a mess. But finally realizing all this, I knew I loved myself enough that I had to walk away.

I think about what I would've done in the past in a situation like this. Walking away from someone you truly love is not easy. And I know the old version of myself would've stayed and continued to allow this person to hurt me. Even though I couldn't imagine them not in my life, letting go was the necessary step forward at the time.

Sometimes the hardest thing to do is often times also the right thing. I had abandoned myself in situations like this before and I knew I couldn't do that to myself again. I deserve to be loved at the highest level. I deserve to be respected, cared for, and protected by the person I love. Not destroyed while they ignore their own demons. It was a hard pill to swallow, and I still think about it every single day. I ask myself how I could stay so long knowing the pain and hurt that it was causing me. Sometimes we look at love and think it's worth the pain. But when you are truly loved by yourself, you won't put yourself in the position I found myself in.

I've come to accept that this relationship was meant to be one of my greatest lessons. I was pushed to test the inner work I had done within myself. All the time I spent learning to love myself again, was faced with the patterns that carefully crafted my entire past. I was shaken to my core and forced to face the ugly truths of who I had once been. I also learned that there are people that will allow you to be your full and truest self. He showed me that I shouldn't be afraid to be who I am. That my emotions are not too much. That sacrifice is often worth it in the end. The greatest gift he gave me was helping me to love myself again. To face uncertainty and pain without abandoning myself. That it's okay to sit in it for a while. To process and understand what it's triggering within you.

Although he has hurt me tremendously, he's been a blessing in my story. This relationship brought me closer to God, in ways I never could have imagined. It gave me opportunities to love others the way I would like to be loved. It taught me that forgiveness is always worth it. That when someone is struggling, be one of the reasons for them not to struggle. I choose to focus on the gains we both had from this relationship and not what was lost. Because in the end, I didn't lose anything. I gained so much more than I ever could have imagined. And when I look back and reflect, I want to thank him for guiding me to this place. I grounded myself in my practice of prayer, surrendering all my worries, fears, and anxiety to Him. There was so much outside of my control and it taught me that we aren't the ones actually in control, that God already has His plans for us and to trust that He will guide you through the path that was meant for you. When I was going through my darkest days, I clung to my newly found faith, and it allowed me to breathe again. This relationship was a testament to all of this, and I wouldn't have been in this place of my faith without it today.

Letting go of someone you love—someone you envisioned spending a life with, someone you thought was your person—can be one of the most painful experiences. I'm still working through it all, but I know that my heart and peace is what I need to focus on protecting right now. To flourish the love I found within myself. And at the end of the day, that's the only love we truly need.

I hope and pray for him every single day. I hope he heals in ways he hasn't been able to in the past. I hope he finds himself along the process, I hope he can be proud of himself and love himself the way I know he deserves. I pray that he finds peace. And that when he looks back at the moment he met me, the moments we shared and the lessons we learned together, that he smiles and is grateful. I hope he finds happiness, in whatever form that will be for him. I don't know what the end of our stories will be, but I hope that it leads us to true happiness, whatever that ends up looking like.

This is a reminder that the love you have for yourself should always be the priority. That when you are whole, you can offer your love to others in a way you could never have imagined. That God put you on this earth to love yourself and love others the way He loves us. That the relationship with yourself is so important. So don't allow yourself to lose it in the process of loving someone else.

Chapter Fifteen

"What do you really have to lose?" I asked myself on that first Sunday morning after my divorce. Standing alone in my empty kitchen, my neighbor's invitation to church hung in the air between us over the phone. After decades of pushing God away, blaming Him for every painful moment of my life, something inexplicable pulled at me. Hours later, I slipped into a back pew, the worship music washing over me like a wave, and felt something I hadn't experienced in years—I felt at home. The irony wasn't lost on me that in my most broken moment, when I had lost everything I thought defined me, I would finally find my way back to Him.

I've shared the journey I have had with my faith throughout my life. Most of it was me being angry at God, resisting His word and feeling like He was absent for most of my life. It wasn't until the tail end of my divorce that I finally opened my heart to Him. I had this neighbor who is a dear friend of mine. She would often invite our family to church with them and we would always decline. I felt like He had been absent in my life for so long, I didn't want to pretend that going to church was where I wanted to be. But during one of the first weekends after my divorce without the kids, I was living alone in my new house, and she reached out and asked if I would join her and her family for church that weekend. I usually declined, but for some reason this time felt different. I thought to myself, "Katie, what do you really have to lose?" So I accepted and met them at one of the services that weekend.

They showed me the children's ministry and the rooms that my boys would attend if we went. Their kids seemed to really love going and it gave me a sense of peace seeing and feeling a sense of community when I walked in. My friend, her husband, and I went to find a spot for the service and when I sat down, an overwhelming sense of relief washed over me. I had been struggling quite a bit and was feeling full of sadness most days, this was one of the first moments I felt at home.

As the message began, they were kicking off a new series called "It Would Take a Miracle." During the introduction, I felt so seen and heard by what was being said. It couldn't have been more relevant to my life than in that exact moment. As I started to attend more services, I soon discovered that each new message felt like it was written just for me. It quickly became the highlight of my weeks. I would go alone, as I often do now, but I've never once felt alone there. I'm realizing now that it is God's presence that is surrounding me to remind me that no one is ever truly alone.

My favorite series to date is one called "Burn The Ships." When it started, I was in a pretty dark place. The message was clear: to move forward, you must fully let go of the past.

You must burn the ships and not look back. They told the story about Lot's wife in the book of Genesis. Lot and his wife were asked to flee their city and were told not to look back. Lot's wife did, though, and she turned to a pillar of salt. The message here is not to look back from our faith but to continue to follow Jesus. This message resonated with me. I often spent my energy focusing on what was behind me. Trying to dissect every last piece of it to try and understand why. But all it was doing was keeping me from moving forward and trusting His plans for me. I learned throughout that series the true meaning of surrender. That to fully trust in Him, we must surrender and know that everything He is doing in our lives has a purpose. Even in the moments when you feel like you are at the bottom of it all, surrender. When you don't know the answer, surrender. When you feel angry about your circumstances, surrender. It was the first time in my life I put my full trust in the Lord. And I can't tell you how freeing that moment was for me. I let go of the control I tried to have over every aspect of my life. Trying to alter the plans He has for me because I was impatient with the lessons. Now, when I'm faced with something difficult, surrender is the first thing I do. There's a lot more peace in your life when you are able to accomplish this.

I started to have the kids join me during their weekends with me, and it's become something we bond over. My kids learn something new every single time they attend, and they love seeing the familiar faces week to week in their program. It brings me immense joy that in a time that has been so hard for all of us, we have something positive keeping us anchored to His love. Once I started to attend regularly, I had a strong desire to start reading more of the Bible. I've done a few self-studies that have helped guide me through certain stories of the Bible. I've found verses that have spoken to me in times where I was flooded with doubt. This was when I really started to dig into my daily practice of prayer.

I was finding that I would pray a lot during times of hardship, but I wanted to make it a daily practice. I wanted to spend time recognizing and showing gratitude for all the amazing things God was blessing me with as well. I had wonderful friends and family who gifted me journals, Bible studies, and daily devotionals that I used to guide my learning and understanding. I still have a long way to go and truly feel no one is ever not learning something from Him. They could have read the Bible from start to finish many times and I still think each time something will resonate with them that hadn't before. I think that is the beauty of God's love and His word. How he is such a teacher to us always. That in order to feel and see His love surround you, you need to surrender to Him and have full faith in His plan for you. This is something that held me back from growing in my faith for a really long time. I couldn't see that despite all the hard times I had faced, that God was behind all of it. Not to make my life hard or difficult, not to cause me pain and heartbreak. It was for Him to prepare me for what He had planned for me. He was using these people, experiences, and hardships to work through me, not against me.

As prayer became a more consistent aspect of my life, that's when I really noticed things start to shift for me. It was a moment to release all the anger I was holding onto. To share my deepest desires for my life and those that I loved. I would have conversations with Him, expressing the pain I felt. Suddenly, as each word of prayer left me, I felt lighter with each word. Years of uncertainty felt peaceful for once. Leaving Him to take on the worries of each day, so I could focus on sharing His love with those around me was what brought purpose to my life again.

A part of one of the messages on surrendering that I often go back to as a reminder is this: "There's a version of your life where you can do something useful and add a lot of value to the people around you. You may not have had great parents, but you can be a great parent. You may not have experienced good leadership, but you can be a good leader. You may not have had a front row seat to a loving and Godly marriage, but I just want you to know you can have one of those. You can have a new life that is so much better than your old life." It gave me all the hope that I am fully capable of living the life God has intended for me.

Now that I've centered myself and my life grounded in my faith, I have seen everything through a different perspective. Through my pain, anger, heartbreak, and confusion over the past couple years, I can see that I show up in those moments as a completely different person. I am much less likely to become angry towards others. I'm able to truly meet people where they are at and feel as though it's my purpose in life as a child of God to extend His love and His word here on earth. I know what it is like to feel so alone and all the times I wish I had someone showing up for me in that way throughout the course of my life. I've come to realize that I can be that person for myself. As I worked through the trials of life after my divorce, I clung to prayer and scripture in those moments when I felt so alone. I turned to Him and witnessed the love He has for me. I use the Bible and His word as my guide. When I don't have all the answers and doubt starts to creep in, I turn to the stories within to bring me comfort. I don't practice prayer just at the end of my days; I give myself the time and grace to pursue that practice whenever my heart leads me there. Knowing He is always with me and there is never the right or wrong time to stop and talk to Him. Now I feel like it's my turn to take my learnings and experiences and offer that to those around me that could find comfort in Him.

Chapter Sixteen

S o where am I today? Realizing I had spent most of my life carrying shame and lacking the vulnerability to be honest—with myself or others—helped me see that by sharing my writing, my experiences, and my healing, there is purpose in our stories. The very stories God has used to shape us. Once I let the vulnerability flow in, I started to see that my life and experiences had a greater impact on others than I ever realized.

Every time I would open myself up to someone, share pieces of my healing journey, or put my writing out there, I would have others reach out to me telling me how much it meant to them. I would get comments like, "I have loved watching this journey you're on. All my love. You're doing amazing work," to, "This is so lovely and brave." It suddenly clicked. My story was full of pain, hurt, anger, and sadness, but what I wasn't seeing is that it was building me to be compassionate, forgiving, empathetic, and trusting. I was so buried underneath the negativity that I couldn't see what the real purpose of all of it was. And to be able to share that with the world has shown me that we are never alone in our struggles.

I've received messages of encouragement when I've been at my lowest. I've had others reach out and share the hope they are gaining by seeing they are not alone in their struggles. I've had people finally finding the strength to face their struggles and work through the hard stuff. Sharing my story has helped me reconnect with others I've lost touch with over the years. It's brought new friendships and relationships into my life. It's been such a blessing, and I'm realizing so clearly that one person's story might save someone else's. This was what God was using me for: to inspire others.

There was a moment when I wanted my writing to reach more people and use it not just as a place for myself to heal, but for others to heal as well. I started a series on my social media platforms called, "The Things We Left Unsaid," to help others tell their stories. Giving voice to the words they so desperately wanted to say but couldn't, crafting it to take their pain and turn it into something beautiful. I'd go through the submissions and allow their words to take me to another place. I'd envision their words and what they were trying to portray. I'd sit down and start drafting poetry based on my understanding of what they shared.

Every time I'd finish a piece, I'd share it with the person who inspired it, hoping that my words would provide them comfort, and a way for them to feel seen and heard. It was something so simple yet divine. I'd get responses like, "Katie this is amazing. Thank you for sharing this, you nailed it," and "I felt every single word. Thank you." I felt so fulfilled by this. Being able to give something to others in a way that brought them a sense of peace. It became my mission to figure out a way to continue sharing more with the world.

Whether that is to inspire them to keep going, to reconnect with their faith, to see others as God sees us and most importantly, to give ourselves that same level of love and compassion. To know that no matter what we are faced with, God is in control, He is always with us, guiding us. And that if you are going through a hard time, He's doing this for a reason—one we may not fully understand in the moment, but one day we will. That's why they call it faith. In Hebrews 11:1 it states, "Now faith is confidence in what we hope for and assurance about what we do not see." It's the best definition I have seen of the word. To hold a space for what is hoped for but trust in God even when we can't see it at the time.

I am not perfect, and I take steps backwards all the time. It's why they call this a journey and not a destination. You may never be fully healed—and that's okay. Because your growth in faith never stops. So it's natural to make mistakes and revert to old habits; we are human after all. But the beautiful thing about that is God will still love you. In times of sadness, confusion, or hurt, this is something I remind myself of repeatedly. It's much easier to forgive yourself when you know that He will still love you and forgives you always. I didn't get there overnight, and I know there are times I question myself or allow others' actions to impact how I view myself still to this day. And I also know that not everyone is on the same journey as I am, and that's okay. It's what keeps us learning from one another. Our purpose in life is not all going to be the same and that's the point.

Just know that we were all created with a purpose, with intention. It's up to you to open your heart, mind, and soul to what that is for you. Once I was able to grasp that, a lot of my uncertainty and anxiety in life went away. Writing this memoir has felt like putting the final stitches in a quilt woven from understanding and forgiveness. There is so much power in fully trusting in His plans for you. To know that He already has your path determined, and instead of fighting it or trying to control it—surrender. Give Him all your worry, your fears, your troubles. He is meant to carry those for you. Because I promise that if He is bringing you to it, He will bring you through it as well.

I'll leave you with this final message: pain isn't punishment—it's preparation. Every challenge and every struggle is shaping us, refining us, and making us stronger for what's to come. I've learned that through my own journey, where the darkest moments ultimately became the groundwork for growth. It's easy to feel defeated when you're in the midst of hardship, but I want you to know that what you're going through is not a sign of failure—it's part of a greater purpose. You are being prepared for something greater, even when it's hard to see. Keep moving forward, because the strength you're building today will carry you into the life you've been waiting for. The light at the end of the tunnel is real—trust that it's worth the walk.

About the Author

Katie M. Schneider lives in Minnesota with her three children. After navigating a childhood marked by family addiction, parental divorce, and the loss of both her sister and mother, she embarked on a journey of healing through therapy, writing, and rekindled faith. Through vulnerability and self-discovery, she transformed her deepest wounds into sources of strength and compassion.

Today, Katie balances motherhood with her passion for creative expression. She enjoys spending time with her children, attending church, embracing an active lifestyle, and building a community through sharing her writing. Her poetry and reflections on healing have resonated with many who recognize their own struggles in her words.

Katie believes that our greatest challenges prepare us for our greatest purpose, and she remains dedicated to helping others find hope in their own journeys. Her story is a testament to the power of forgiveness, faith, and the courage to begin again.

 instagram.com/kmschneids

www.ingramcontent.com/pod-product-compliance
Lightning Source LLC
Chambersburg PA
CBHW031532120626
46545CB00005B/2111